Critical Guides to Spanish Texts

Critical Guides to Spanish Texts

EDITED BY J. E. VAREY AND A. D. DEYERMOND

30 Pérez Galdós: La de Bringas

Critical Guides to Spanish Texts

EDITED BY J. E. VAREY AND A. D. DEYERMOND

PÉREZ GALDÓS

La de Bringas

Peter Bly

Associate Professor of Spanish,
Queen's University, Kingston, Ontario

Grant & Cutler Ltd *in association with*
Tamesis Books Ltd 1981

© Grant & Cutler Ltd
1981
ISBN 0 7293 0110 9

I.S.B.N. 84-499-5164-X

DEPÓSITO LEGAL: V. 2.825 - 1981

Printed in Spain by
Artes Gráficas Soler, S. A. - La Olivereta, 28 - Valencia (18)
for
GRANT AND CUTLER LTD
11 BUCKINGHAM STREET, LONDON, W.C.2

Contents

Abbreviations

For my parents,
Mollie and Phillip Bly

Preface

REFERENCES to the text of *La de Bringas* are from the edition by Federico Carlos Sainz de Robles in *Obras completas* (Madrid: Aguilar, 1969), pp. 1585-1683; they indicate the chapter number followed by the page number, thus: XLI, 1664, Whilst the best separate edition is that of Ricardo Gullón *(21)*, with its most useful introduction, I have preferred Robles's edition because of its greater accessibility. References to *Tormento* and *Marianela* are from the same volume; quotations from Galdós's non-fictional writings are from Volume VI (1968), unless otherwise stated.

The figures in parentheses in italic type refer to the numbered items in the Bibliographical Note; where necessary these are followed by page numbers, thus: *16,* p. 276.

I should like to acknowledge the generous assistance of the Advisory Research Committee II, School of Graduate Studies and Research, Queen's University, which awarded me a research and typing grant; and of Dr Leo J. Hoar, Jr, and Dr Anthony Percival, who provided research materials.

I am also very grateful to Professors J. E. Varey and A. D. Deyermond, the editors of this series, for their kind and helpful comments on the draft of this book.

Finally, I should like to thank Ms Kathy Doyle for her careful typing of the text and also my wife and children for their patience and understanding during its preparation.

P. A. B.

1. Introduction

*L*A *de Bringas* was completed in May 1884, 'ese año mila-
groso' of literary activity *(16,* p. 120) in which Galdós
also produced *Tormento* (in January), Part I of *Lo prohibido*
(in November) and his first series of regular fortnightly con-
tributions to the Buenos Aires newspaper, *La Prensa.* A number of literary critics, both at the time and since, have tended
to regard *La de Bringas* as part of Galdós's Naturalist period
which had begun in 1881 with the publication of *La desheredada.* Such was the opinion of Luis Alfonso, who in his July
1884 review wrote: 'La evolución iniciada en *La desheredada*
y conducida a su última expresión en *La de Bringas,* no hay
que decir si llenó de júbilo a unos cuantos, que aunque pocos,
suenan mucho' [i.e., the Naturalists] *(24).* Stronger words were
used by Cristóbal Botella three months later: *'El doctor Centeno, Tormento* y *La de Bringas* son los frutos que ha produ-
cido la poderosa inteligencia de Galdós, sometida a las mez-
quinas leyes del naturalismo artístico' *(25).* In more recent
times, this criticism has been repeated in general surveys of
Galdós's work *(4;6).*

Such a facile categorization is comprehensible given the
historical context of *La de Bringas*'s publication. A year earlier,
when the bitter polemic aroused by French Naturalism in Spanish literary circles had reached a climax with Pardo Bazán's
triumphant defence of Naturalism in *La cuestión palpitante,*
Galdós had been the object of an enthusiastic testimonial dinner
organized by Leopoldo Alas, Palacio Valdés and other Naturalist supporters in the Café Inglés in Madrid. [1] Their partisan,
though unsuccessful, support of Galdós's candidacy for a vacant
seat in the Real Academia Española the same year, followed

---

[1] Walter T. Pattison, *El naturalismo español: historia externa de
un movimiento literario* (Madrid: Gredos, 1965), pp. 94-6.

in 1884 by the first publication of French translations of his early work, also contributed to the misconception that Galdós was a faithful imitator of Zola. Don Benito's own cryptic remarks during this period and later were singularly unhelpful. In a personal letter to Giner de los Ríos a year after the publication of *La desheredada,* he used words which could be interpreted as a reference to the adoption of Naturalism: 'Efectivamente, yo he querido en esta obra entrar por nuevo camino o inaugurar mi segunda o tercera *manera,* como se dice de los pintores. Puse en ello especial empeño, y desde que concluí el tomo, lo tuve por superior a todo lo que he hecho anteriormente.'[2] A similar lack of complete candour is noticeable in his 1901 prologue to *La Regenta*: 'Escribió Alas su obra en tiempos no lejanos, cuando andábamos en aquella procesión del Naturalismo, marchando hacia el templo del arte con menos pompa retórica de la que antes se usaba, abandonadas las vestiduras caballerescas, y haciendo gala de la ropa usada en los actos comunes de la vida' (*7,* p. 214). Even though the Naturalist label may be a convenient method of classifying *La de Bringas* in relation to the corpus of Galdós's work, it really does not aid the modern reader to understand the novel's complex composition and meaning, nor indeed is it relevant, for environment and heredity, the twin pillars of Naturalist ideology, do not play as important a part as one would expect to find in the work of a committed Naturalist author. None the less, other, less substantive, aspects of the Naturalist novel as perceived by its opponents can serve as a useful starting point for our efforts to discover the true meaning of Galdós's fifth novel of the *serie contemporánea.*

One charge levelled by Alfonso was that the subject matter of *La de Bringas,* like that of most Naturalist novels, was trivial: 'Toda la vulgar Ilíada de *La de Bringas* cabe anchamente en una copla popular que en estos mismos días he oído:

> Mujer que viste de seda
> Sin permitirlo el caudal,

    [2] Letter of 14 April 1882, reproduced in M. B. Cossío, 'Galdós y Giner. Una carta de Galdós', *La Lectura,* XX (1920), 254-8 (at p. 257).

> Yo no digo que lo sea...
> Pero quizá lo será...

Y la glosa de este cantar estaba, lo repito, trazada de modo que no había menester añadiduras ni ampliaciones, en *Tormento*' *(24)*. Orlando was also categorical about the unsuitability of this material: '*La de Bringas,* ni por el asunto, ni por los personajes, debía figurar al lado de las novelas publicadas hasta ahora por tan preclaro ingenio. Después de leer este libro acuden inmediatamente estas preguntas: ¿Para qué se habrá pretendido hacer con materiales tan ínfimos y deleznables una novela?' *(26,* p. 444). And if we are to believe the testimony of both critics, this opinion was shared by booksellers and the general reading public. In short, *La de Bringas* just did not appeal, because of its apparently monotonous, simple subject matter. Alfonso adds: 'y en efecto, ¿cómo había de gustar un libro pesado? Porque éste es el calificativo vulgar, pero gráfico, que se ha aplicado a la novela, por cuanto en sus 227 páginas no hay otro tema que las trampas, enredos y bellaquerías de la protagonista para gastar más en trapos y moños de lo que puede' *(24)*. If these charges are valid, then, indeed, Galdós's purpose in composing *La de Bringas* is seriously called in question.

The second criticism that stands out in both reviews is Galdós's excessive use of detail. Alfonso relates how 'la manía de la menudencia y el pormenor, encanto de la escuela naturalista, empezó a causar sus estragos en Pérez Galdós' *(24)*. Orlando's criticism is more colourfully worded: 'Unos no han podido salir del laberinto en que Pérez y su acompañante se meten en busca de Don Francisco Bringas; a otros se les ha atragantado el cuadro de pelo que éste fabrica ... muchas personas de ambos sexos se han visto punto menos que ahogados entre tanta cinta, tanto lazo y tanto trapo, y mareados por el bulle bulle y el ir y venir de la misma persona siempre con el mismo objeto y persiguiendo el mismo fin' *(26,* p. 444). Even contemporary admirers (apparently very few) felt that the material descriptions were somewhat excessive. Picón referred to the novel as 'el último estudio social de Galdós, cuajado de

detalles' *(27)*. Alas felt that 'sobran algunos capítulos.'[3] Galdós's
attention to microscopic detail (in Francisco Ynduráin's quaint
phrase: his 'afán enumerativo y cosista'[4]) is a constant feature
of his novels as Menéndez y Pelayo indicated in his 1897 Real
Academia reply to Galdós.[5] But why did Galdós decide to
indulge this interest to such a degree in a novel which did not
possess in the first instance a story-line powerful enough, or so
it seemed, to hold the readers' attention? Surely Galdós was
only adding to his problems by dwelling so unnecessarily on
the description of minutiae. These two undeniable aspects of
La de Bringas — prosaic subject matter and an accumulation
of detail — will remain serious indictments of Galdós's poor
literary skill, if it is not convincingly demonstrated that they
fulfill a perfectly logical and appropriate function in the overall
aim of the novel. In fact, these two aspects lead us to the heart
of Galdós's concept of his literary art. Throughout his career,
even before the advent of the Naturalism polemic in the early
1880s, Galdós always emphasized the importance of the novelist's correct observation of the external, visible world. In his
first literary manifesto, 'Observaciones sobre la novela contemporánea en España', he had strenuously rebutted the claim by
foreigners that Spanish writers were 'unos idealistas desafora-
dos, y más nos agrada imaginar que observar' by pointing to
the example of Cervantes, asserting that 'la aptitud existe en
nuestra raza; pero sin duda esta degeneración lamentable en
que vivimos, nos la eclipsa y sofoca' (*7*, pp. 116-17). His
inaugural speech to the Real Academia contains the fullest
declaration of his aesthetic principles:

> Imagen de la vida es la Novela, y el arte de componerla
> estriba en reproducir los caracteres humanos, las pasio-
> nes, las debilidades, lo grande y lo pequeño, las almas
> y las fisonomías, todo lo espiritual y lo físico que nos

[3] Letter dated 24 July 1884, reproduced by Soledad Ortega, *Cartas
a Galdós* (Madrid: Revista de Occidente, 1964), p. 222.
[4] *Galdós entre la novela y el folletín* (Madrid: Taurus, 1970), p. 55.
[5] Reproduced in 'Don Benito Pérez Galdós', in *Estudios y discursos
de crítica histórica y literaria*, V (Madrid: Consejo Superior de Investigaciones Científicas, 1942), pp. 81-103 (at p. 98).

constituye y nos rodea, y el lenguaje, que es la marca de raza, y las viviendas, que son el signo de familia, y la vestidura, que diseña los últimos trazos externos de la personalidad: *todo esto sin olvidar que debe existir perfecto fiel de balanza entre la exactitud y la belleza de la reproducción.* (my italics; 7, pp. 175-6)

These confessions of technique have undoubtedly encouraged the generalization that the most important facet of Galdós's novelistic style is his faithful reproduction of contemporary observable reality. The views of Guillermo Díaz-Plaja and Francisco Monterde are representative: 'Galdós ofrece la visión de la realidad por el escritor tal como se presenta a nuestros ojos.' [6] Yet this interpretation of Galdós's works ignores the equally important stress that Galdós put in the above declaration on the artistic beauty of the literary recreation of reality. Later in the same year of 1897, on the occasion of Pereda's entry into the Real Academia he was to repeat: 'Lo que importa es que el artista sepa encontrar la desnudez humana, y acierte a ornarla con el colorido local *sin que sus bellezas se pierdan*' (my italics, 7, p. 196). Even as early as the 1870 manifesto, he had praised Ruiz Aguilera's short stories for the successful combination of these two fundamental artistic aims: 'Son tan naturales [the characters] que les conocemos desde que salen, y al punto les relacionamos con alguien que va por ahí tan serio sin pensar que un arte habilísimo ha expresado al vuelo su fisonomía *con la rapidez de la fotografía y la belleza de la pintura*' (my italics, 7, pp. 131-2). The novelist had to draw his material from the real experiences of life but equally important, he had to give that material artistic shape, order it so that it was aesthetically pleasing to the reader. This surely must be the meaning of his term 'belleza'. Moreover, far from appearing antagonistic, the two concepts of fidelity ('fotografía') and artistic elaboration ('belleza') are mutually dependent in the perfect novel, the one quality inseparable from the other. Galdós was essentially an artist, conscious of his art and

---

6 *Historia de la literatura española e historia de la literatura mexicana,* 4th ed. (México: Porrúa, 1965), p. 331.

its relationship to the chaotic flow of life from which he drew his material. Consequently, it is in the context of these permanent artistic preoccupations of Galdós that the two supposed weaknesses of composition in *La de Bringas* have to be considered.

Perhaps it is significant that in his *Memorias de un desmemoriado* (1916) he did not remember the period of *La de Bringas*'s publication as one of Naturalist imitation, but rather of pure artistic creativity: 'Después de *La familia de León Roch*, y sin respiro, *La desheredada;* en seguida me metí con *El amigo Manso, El doctor Centeno, Tormento, La de Bringas* y *Lo prohibido*... Hallábame yo por entonces en la plenitud de la fiebre novelesca' (p. 1676). With *El doctor Centeno* and *Tormento* Galdós had commenced a series of interconnected social novels. The results were not totally successful: characterization and thematic unity were singled out as deficiencies along with the Naturalist features noted above (*23*, pp. 122-4). [7] Thus, when he started on the third component of this sub-series, Galdós was very much aware of weaknesses in his technique. For most of the critics, these weaknesses were still evident in *La de Bringas*. But more discriminating critics felt that they had been overcome: *La de Bringas* was, indeed, an improvement. The enthusiastic Alas wrote to Galdós: 'basta ahora decir que es de las [novelas suyas] que me gustaron más.' [8] Picón was equally effusive: 'Bien quisiera, tratando de justificar los elogios, alabar todo lo bueno que tiene, a mi juicio, *La de Bringas,* pero no debo hacerlo' (*27*). José Castro y Serrano, who claimed some part in the novel's genesis, reckoned that 'quizá en ninguno [escrito] ha derramado tanta gracia, tanta naturalidad y tan fluidos conceptos como en *La de Bringas*' (letter of 22 July 1884, *16*, p. 278). The French critic Tréverret correctly pointed

---

[7] David Cluff (*30*) has tried, successfully, to rebut these criticisms. A persuasive rehabilitation of *El doctor Centeno* has also recently been achieved by Geraldine M. Scanlon, 'El doctor Centeno: a Study in Obsolescent Values', *Bulletin of Hispanic Studies*, LV (1978), 245-53.

[8] *Cartas a Galdós*, p. 222.

to the marked contrast between the brevity of the composition period and the appreciable improvement in Galdós's style. [9]

The artistic excellence of *La de Bringas,* that perfect fusion of 'fotografía' and 'belleza' which Galdós constantly aimed at, far from being less appreciated with time, has caused many modern critics to hail *La de Bringas* as one of Galdós's masterpieces. Montesinos termed it 'novela excepcional en todo' (*16,* p. 139). V. S. Pritchett thought it 'a brilliant, well-constructed comic story' (*41,* p. 32), an opinion echoed almost in the same words by Gerald Brenan (*22,* p. 12). Furthermore, the notion that *La de Bringas* is a novel with relevance even for the technological world of the twentieth century has been put forward by Ricardo Gullón (*14,* p. 112), Pritchett (*41,* p. 36) and Gregorio Marañón. [10] However, the same paradoxical situation that surrounded the novel's first reception still seems to obtain: though a minority of literary critics and students wax enthusiastic, the general literary reviewer and reader (in Spain, at least) continues to ignore it (*16,* p. 152).

In short, the need to demonstrate conclusively the supreme artistic skill with which Galdós shaped his ordinary raw material in *La de Bringas* remains as urgent as ever. By means of chapters devoted to the novel's structure, setting, characterization, language, social pictures, political background and narrative technique, this guide will attempt to satisfy that need. I hope it will show not only that Galdós integrated all the raw material at his disposal into a coherent and meaningful work of art, but also that the format of that artistic recreation, reflecting life's ambiguity, allows *La de Bringas* to transcend time and space. No greater 'belleza' could be asked from a fictional 'fotografía'. To aid the reader in this voyage of discovery Galdós deliberately positions in the first three chapters one of the most apparently gratuitous descriptions he ever composed, but which on closer inspection sums up the whole novel's content, theme and style.

[9] 'La Littérature espagnole contemporaine. Le Roman et le réalisme. III. M. Pérez Galdós', *Le Correspondant* (10 April 1885), pp. 150-67 (at p. 167).

[10] 'El mundo por la claraboya', *Obras completas,* IV (Madrid: Aguilar, 1968), pp. 867-70 (at p. 870).

2. *Perspective and vision*

FRANCISCO Bringas's hair-picture is a work of visual perspective. The surface design presents a foreground filled with elegiac objects, whilst the background 'consistía en el progresivo alejamiento de otros sauces de menos talla que se iban ... camino del horizonte' (I, 1587). The illusion of spatial perspective on a flat surface is increased by the colour gradation and proximity of the hairs. The work's physical shape is also three-dimensional: different layers of materials are used in the picture's composition. The hairs, of various sizes, have been glued onto a glass lens fixed over a pencilled outline of the design, which is itself attached to a wooden base. However, this three-dimensional perspective is not normal: the final frame of a convex lens ensures that the whole work cannot be appreciated in its proper perspective. This distortion only continues that of the surface design of the picture where the foreground is crowded with small objects like flowers, bats, urns: 'Estos objetos se encaramaban unos sobre otros, cual si se disputasen, pulgada a pulgada, el sitio que habían de ocupar' (I, 1587). Yet in the background much larger objects (mountains, a city, the moon and the sea) are depicted in vague, blurred outlines:

> Más allá veíanse suaves contornos de montañas que ondulaban ... ; luego había un poco de mar, otro poco de río, el confuso perfil de una ciudad con góticas torres y almenas; y arriba, en el espacio destinado al cielo, una oblea que debía de ser la Luna, a juzgar por los blancos reflejos de ella que esmaltaban las aguas y los montes. (I, 1587)

Thus, in design and execution, the hair-picture is an object of confusing perspectives, an optical illusion.

Appropriately, in its initial presentation to the reader, the true identity of the object emerges only after a succession of confusing paragraphs. The narrator's first words suggest that he is looking at a real (albeit bizarre) object: 'Era aquello..., ¿cómo lo diré yo?..., un gallardo artificio sepulcral de atrevidísima arquitectura' (I, 1587). The second paragraph, with its discussion of the Romantic fashion for the decorative willow tree, causes some uneasiness. However, it is only at the beginning of paragraph three that we learn that this object is part of an artistic representation, the exact nature of which the narrator still cannot determine: '¿Era talla dulce, aguafuerte, plancha de acero, boj o pacienzuda obra ejecutada a punta de lápiz duro o con pluma a la tinta china?' (I, 1587). There is more description of the picture's component lines and dots before the narrator finally discloses at the end of the chapter: 'Era, en fin, el tal cenotafio un trabajo de pelo o en pelo, género de arte que tuvo cierta boga' (I, 1588). [11] What first appears to be a real tomb of ordinary proportions turns out to be a miniature artistic reproduction composed of human hair. This almost absurd reduction of opposing physical dimensions is emphasized by the narrator's praise of Francisco's innovative skill: '¡Qué diablo de hombre! Habría sido capaz de hacer un rosario de granos de arena, si se pone a ello, o de reproducir la catedral de Toledo en una cáscara de avellana' (III, 1590; the same reconciliation of opposing dimensions is achieved in Isabelita's first nightmare when she feels the whole Palace and its inhabitants inside her stomach). This *reductio ad absurdum* is also represented by the change in style of the narrator. The list of the various classical features of the mausoleum ends with a reference to the contemporary decoration of a street kiosk. In the same way the grandiose relation of the tomb's inscription ends with an absurdly vulgar image: 'Publi-

---

[11] He subsequently adds that such objects 'ya sólo se ven marchitas y sucias, en el escaparate de anticuados peluqueros o en algunos nichos de campo santo' (II, 1588). F. Nevill Jackson, *Ancestors in Silhouette Cut by August Edouart* (London: The Bodley Head, 1921), p. 3, places the vogue for hair-work between 1813 and 1825. Palley (*40*, p. 339) notes the mention of a hair-picture in *Madame Bovary*. See also Augustin Edouart, *A Treatise on Silhouette Likenesses* (London: Longman, 1835), pp. 52-3, for a description of the technique of hair-painting.

caban desconsoladamente sus nombres diversas letras compungidas, de cuyos trazos inferiores salían unos lagrimones que figuraban resbalar por el mármol al modo de babas escurridizas' (I, 1587) (see *14*, pp. 130-1).

The retrospective account of the hair-picture's composition given in Chapters II and III continues this process of progressively unmasking the truly vulgar nature of the work. Its basic design is an absurd hotch-potch of incongruent shapes and objects culled indiscriminately from a variety of sources:

> No gustándole ninguno de los dibujos de monumento fúnebre que en su colección tenía, resolvió hacer uno; mas como no le daba el naipe por la invención, compuso, con partes tomadas de obras diferentes, el bien trabado conjunto... Procedía el sauce de *La tumba de Napoleón en Santa Elena*; el ángel que hacía pucheros había venido del túmulo que pusieron en El Escorial para los funerales de una de las mujeres de Fernando VII, y la lontananza fue tomada de un grabadito de no sé qué librote lamartinesco que era todo un puro jarabe. Finalmente, las flores las cosechó Bringas en el jardín de un libro ilustrado sobre el *Lenguaje* de las tales que provenía de la biblioteca de doña Cándida. (III, 1590)

Francisco's absurdly ecstatic visions of the completed object (II, 1589) are accordingly put into proper perspective by this revelation.

However, the hair-picture continues to perplex the reader beyond the first three chapters. Our initial impression that it is a completed picture is gradually undermined by subsequent reports from the narrator: 'Todo el mes de marzo [de 1868] se lo llevó en el cenotafio y en el sauce, cuyas hojas fueron brotando una por una, y a mediados de abril tenía el ángel brazos y cabeza' (III, 1590). In May Francisco is proceeding 'en la febril, aunque ordenada marcha de su trabajo' (XII, 1606). By the beginning of June 'el ángel estaba completamente modelado ya... El sauce protegía con sus llorosas ramas la tumba... Al fondo nada le faltaba ya; era un modelo de perspectiva melancólica... Faltaban aún las flores del piso y todo el primer término, *donde Bringas discurrió a última hora* poner unas columnas rotas y caídas, así como de templo en ruinas' (my italics; XVII, 1616). The addition of the columns at this late stage implies that the original observation by the narrator must have been made at some unspecified time between March and June. By the beginning of September Francisco has recovered sufficiently to recommence his picture, but the outbreak of the Revolution upsets his plans. So, it is only at the end of the novel (XLVIII, 1679) that we realize that the description, so minutely and definitively recorded on the first page, is really incomplete. Confusion, ultimately dispelled only after a process of successive revelations, thus accompanies the presentation of the hair-picture throughout the novel.

Critics have had no difficulty in relating this apparently gratuitous pictorial emblem to the themes and structure of the rest of the novel. Gullón saw the chaotic picture as a miniature reproduction of the Palace labyrinth (*14*, p. 113). Others have regarded it as an emblem of the hollow values held by the Bringas family, their friends and the Bourbon régime (*9*, p. 93; *40*, p. 348; *46*, p. 63). Pritchett (*41*, p. 33) even reckons that it is another manifestation of the eternal Spanish preoccupation with death. The hair-picture does succinctly sum up many, perhaps all, aspects of the novel; it is a 'microcosmos' (X, 1601), representing, and represented in turn by, other objects, attitudes, behaviour. It is the first of a series of Chinese boxes that make up the novel's thematic texture, as I hope to show in the following chapters. Moreover, it is the core of the novel, for without this little objet d'art, *La de Bringas* would not have developed as it does. With its importance in inverse proportion to its physical size, the hair-picture, finally, offers an object lesson to the reader in his attempt to unravel the novel's meaning: the surface appearance of the novel (whether at the thematic, structural, chronological or linguistic level) conceals a third dimension of inner truth whose depths have to be plumbed.

Galdós does not limit his lesson in optical illusions to the nature of the object viewed (in this case, the hair-picture). He examines other possible factors, amongst which the physical distance separating object and spectator is especially important. In an attempt to find their own way to the Bringas apartment, Pez and the narrator plot a course through the Palace corridors

by looking out of the window at the Chapel cupola (IV, 1592).
Greater confusion is the only result as the cupola disappears
behind other structures. The view of the Plaza de Oriente from
the large balcony on the third floor of the servants' quarters
demonstrates the dangerous extremes of visual distortion produced when an excessive distance separates viewer and object:
'El caballo de Felipe IV nos parecía un juguete, el Teatro Real
una barraca y el plano superior del cornisamento de Palacio
un ancho puente sobre el precipicio, por donde podría correr
con holgura quien no padeciera vértigos' (IV, 1593). The soar-
ing, angled flights of the pigeons 'a quienes veíamos precipitarse
en el hondo abismo de la plaza ... y subir luego *en velocísima
curva* a posarse en los capiteles y en las molduras' (my italics)
underline this process of distortion as well as referring the
reader back to the convex lens placed over the hair-picture.
In the Maundy Thursday scenes in the Chapel and the Salón
de Columnas in Chapter VIII distortion of the physical object
is now produced by a restricted viewing aperture as well as an
abnormal distance separating viewer and object (*34*):

> Como eran amigas del sacristán ... [the girls] pudieron
> colocarse en la escalera de la capilla hasta *vislumbrar,
> por entre puertas entornadas,* la mitra del patriarca y dos
> velas apagadas del tenebrario, un altar cubierto de tela
> morada, algunas calvas de capellanes y algunos pechos
> de gentileshombres cargados de cruces y bandas; pero
> nada más. Poco más tarde *lograron ver algo* de la her-
> mosa ceremonia de dar la comida a los pobres después
> del lavatorio. Hay en el ala meridional de la terraza *unas
> grandes claraboyas de cristales,* protegidas por redes de
> alambre ... por ellas, se ve tan de cerca el curvo techo,
> que resultan monstruosas y groseramente pintadas las
> figuras que lo decoran. Angelones y ninfas extienden por
> la escocia sus piernas enormes, cabalgando sobre nubes
> que semejan pacas de algodón. De otras figuras cree-
> ríase que con el esfuerzo de su colosal musculatura le-
> vantan en vilo la armazón del techo. En cambio, las flores
> de la alfombra, que se ve en lo profundo, tomaríanse por
> miniaturas. (my italics; VIII, 1598)

The apertures in the 'claraboyas' are made even smaller by the jostling spectators. Wanting to gain a closer view of the ceremony, they only succeed in viewing a more distorted and partial image: if the table of the twelve male beggars is indistinct, every feature of the twelve females is clearly viewed. The grotesque dimensions of the angels on the ceiling, the miniature flowers on the carpet and the curvature of the ceiling itself, recalling elements in the hair-picture, indicate the degree of distortion produced by an abnormal viewing aperture and distance.

Even if the angles of vision were not abnormally vertical and the windows were not barriers in the above examples, the quality of light would still be another important factor (*47*) determining the exactness of the viewed image: Francisco's working space is very well lit by the bright sunshine entering the window on the Campo del Moro side of the Palace, but the interior rooms of the Bringas household are murkily lit with an arrangement of patches of alternating light and darkness that is repeated in the corridors: 'De trecho en trecho encontrábamos espacios ... inundados de luz solar, la cual entraba por grandes huecos abiertos al patio. La claridad del día, reflejada por las paredes blancas, penetraba a lo largo de los pasadizos ..., se perdía y se desmayaba en ellos, hasta morir completamente a la vista de los rojizos abanicos del gas' (IV, 1591).

One final factor has to be considered: the ability of the viewer to see the physical object correctly, given the reliability of the other determining factors. The initial description of the hair-picture had firmly established the existence of a person viewing the physical object, a viewer who was not, however, completely certain of what he saw or that he could describe it: 'Era aquello ..., ¿cómo lo diré yo?'; the reader is shortly afterwards enlisted as another spectator: 'Reparad en lo nimio, escrupuloso y firme de tan difícil trabajo' (I, 1587). Galdós returns to the question of the viewer's relation to the object half-way through the novel, showing that the viewer's physical and emotional condition can also determine the accurary of the visual image of external reality: the narrator, feeling the soporific effects of the conversation at Tula's tertulia, of the sunlight filtering through the windows, of the swishing of fans and the rocking of chairs, experiences a condition 'semejante al que los médicos llaman *coma vigil,* un ver sin ver, transición de imagen a fantasmas, un oír sin oír, mezcla de son y zumbido' (XXVII, 1637). A somewhat similar scene occurs towards the end when Rosalía, drawn to the Prado tertulias by her desperate need to secure funds, reviews the sexual and financial possibilities of male passers-by:

> Observando en la semioscuridad del Prado la procesional marea de paseantes, veía pasar algunas personas, muy contadas, *que atraían la atención de su exaltado espíritu.* El farol más próximo las iluminaba lo bastante para reconocerlas; después se perdían en la sombra polvorosa. Vio al marqués de Fúcar, que había vuelto ya de Biarritz, orondo, craso, todo forrado de billetes de Banco; a Onésimo, que solía mirar como suyo el Tesoro Público; a Trujillo, el banquero; a Mompous, al agente de Bolsa don Buenaventura de Lantigua, y otros. De estos poderosos unos la conocían; otros, no; algunos de ellos habíanle dirigido tal cual vez miradas que debían de ser amorosas. Otros eran de intachables costumbres dentro y fuera de su casa. (my italics; XLI, 1665).

The distance and semi-darkness, far from being an impediment for the somnolent viewer, now become a stimulus for the active mind or imagination. Bent on one idea, this perceptive internal vision, nevertheless, is still selective, partial, incomplete: all other human qualities are ignored as the imagination focusses on one particular trait.

The most substantial methodological lesson in perspective and vision is provided, of course, by the case-history of Francisco's blindness, a result of the excessive work on that optical illusion, the hair-picture, and the major determinant of the course of the novel. Francisco prizes his very good eyesight above all other physical faculties: 'lo primero es la salud, y lo primero de la salud, la vista' (XXXVIII, 1657), a belief voiced earlier by the narrator (XXX, 1643) and Rosalía (XXV, 1633). However, he fails to heed the warnings of blindness from his friends and children. The progress of his illness (attack, partial recovery of vision, relapse, firmer recovery, final setback), its diagnosis and treatment are presented in a series of stages mirroring the perspectivism of the hair-picture.[12] When considered in the light of other ophthalmological cases mentioned by Cándida (XX, 1622), Torres (XXI, 1624) and Francisco himself (XXV, 1642; XXXII, 1646), the latter's illness, with its successive ups and downs, is not as permanent or as traumatic an event as Francisco would have us believe. One also wonders how vital his eyesight is for his normal, daily functions (its loss is, of course, an impediment for his hair-work): for, although bandaged and immobilized, he is still able to direct the domestic routine with his usual authority (XXV, 1633), perceive events and people with his well-developed sense of hearing and count his money with his equally reliable sense of touch: 'sus dedos debían de ser dedos del céfiro que acaricia las flores sin ajarlas' (III, 1590). Life seems to continue much as before for Francisco. A partial return of eyesight is sufficient for him to correctly see before him the physical reality of Rosalía's new peignoir: 'Es un consuelo ver de rato en rato alguna cosilla, aunque sólo sea la cavidad de la habitación, con los objetos confusos y como borrados; es consuelo verte, y por cierto que si no me engaña esta pícara retina enferma, tienes puesta una bata de seda' (XXII, 1627). However, he refuses to believe the physical evidence of his eyes and accepts Rosalía's hurried excuse for this extravagant purchase. This scene indeed reinforces the significance of the earlier confrontation when, before his attack of blindness, Francisco had surprised Rosalía at her clandestine dress-making: 'Peeero mujer, ¿qué es esto? —dijo Thiers, absorto, *como quien ve cosas sobrenaturales o mágicas y no da crédito a sus ojos*' (my italics; XV, 1611). The point is that Francisco's physical ability, the advantages of which are deba-

---

[12] First diagnosed by the doctor as 'congestión retiniana' (XXII, 1622), the illness is later certified by the specialist Golfín as conjunctivitis. The bandaging, cauterisation with silver nitrate, saline, copper sulphate and belladonna (XXXII, 1646) is the correct medical treatment for the period; see Daniel M. Albert and Harold G. Scheie, *A History of Ophthalmology at the University of Pennsylvania* (Springfield, Illinois: Charles C. Thomas, 1965), Chapter V: 'Treatment of the Eye in the Mid-Nineteenth Century' (pp. 83-106).

table when only applied to the creation of the hair-picture, is
not matched by a corresponding penetration of mental or spiritual insight. He cannot perceive the significance of those physical images. A later semi-confession to Rosalía reveals that
this inner blindness is also, in part, deliberate, self-induced:
'Me parecía que te salías algo de nuestro régimen tradicional.
Pero teniendo en cuenta tus virtudes, *cierro mis ojos a aquella
disparatada ostentación*' (my italics; XLI, 1665). In *Tormento*
this lack of insight had been singled out as a dominant trait:
'No faltaba en Bringas más que el mirar profundo y todo lo
que es de la peculiar fisonomía del espíritu' (II, 1477) (see also
17, 46). However, on a limited number of occasions Francisco
can be surprisingly perceptive as, for example, when he warns
Refugio about the dangers of the fashion trade: '¡Bonito ne-
gocio! ¡Vaya unos micos que te van a dar tus parroquianas!
Aquí el lujo está en razón inversa del dinero con que pagarlo.
Mucho ojo, niña' (XXVI, 1636). The irony of this percepti-
veness is that its results are not applied, as they should be, to
Francisco's own family situation. On the other hand, Francisco
does possess another type of inner vision: imagination; but it
is so highly developed that it obliterates his embryonic moral
insight. His alarming tendency to superimpose this inner vision
on external reality is evident from the opening chapters: 'su
fantasía se regalaba de antemano con la imagen de la obra
[the hair-picture], figurándosela ya parida y palpitante, com-
pleta, acabada, con la forma del molde en que estuviera. Otras
veces veíala nacer por partes, asomando ahora un miembro,
luego otro, hasta que toda entera aparecía en el reino de la
luz' (II, 1589). Political developments also encourage this
weakness so that he completely misreads the real nature of the
forthcoming revolution: 'Ya verás, ya verás la que se arma
si triunfa esa canalla' (XLIII, 1669). This absurd prophecy is
put into proper perspective by Cándida's comments on the
militia take-over of the Palace: 'En fin es una risa. Baje usted
y verá, verá' (XLIX, 1681).

Rosalía displays the same propensity to subordinate moral
or spiritual introspection to a flattering fantasy. Danger signals
are sounded early when she stands enraptured by Milagros's
dress-making plans: 'Contemplando en éxtasis lo que aún no

es más que una abstracción' (X, 1602). The great temptation to buy new dresses is represented as a visual experience: 'el género le entraba por el ojo derecho' (XXXVIII, 1659). She often imagines people standing before her (Agustín Caballero, XXXIX, 1660; Torres, XVIII, 1618), or visualizes resorts like Arcachon (XXXIX, 1661). Towards the end of the novel, she envisages the series of future lovers: 'se figuraba estar tendiendo sus redes en mares anchos y batidos ... Su mente soñadora la llevaba a los días del próximo invierno' (XLVIII, 1679). Like her husband, Rosalía shows an occasional flash of moral insight when reviewing the ostentation of Milagros (XIV, 1609-10) and Pez (XXXI, 1643-4) (see *38*) but never in relation to her own predicament. This inability is continually emphasized during her desperate visit to Refugio, now the sole hope for financial help: '¿A quién volver los ojos?' (XLI, 1664; XLIV, 1671). Rosalía is astounded at the disorder of the room and she notes the insistent gaze of Refugio (XLVI, 1673-5) but fails to apply Refugio's moral lesson to her conduct or see the reflection of her own disordered sewing quarters in her cousin's room. Significantly, our last picture of Rosalía is of a silent but wide-eyed woman: 'de sus ojos elocuentes se desprendía una convicción orgullosa, la conciencia de su papel de piedra angular de la casa en tan aflictivas circunstancias' (L, 1683). Physical sight, unaccompanied by moral reflection, is directed to possible customers as she regales the narrator with 'miradas un tanto flamígeras' (L, 1683). A similar amoral projection comes from Pez's eyes, 'españoles netos, de una serenidad y dulzura tales, que recordaban los que Murillo supo pintar interpretando a San José' (XII, 1607); they are very similar to the glass eyes of Isabelita's dolls (VII, 1598). Fantasy has replaced moral insight: 'Considerábase superior a sus contemporáneos, al menos veía más, columbraba otra cosa mejor, y como no lograra llevarla a la realidad, de aquí su flemática calma ... Para contemplar en su fantasía la regeneración de España, apartaba los ojos de la corrupción de las costumbres' (XXVII, 1637).

Other characters directly involved in the story of Francisco's loss of sight also contribute to Galdós's examination of the question of true vision: the brilliant oculist Golfín displays a moral obtuseness or short-sightedness when, judging from the Bringas's

public ostentation, he concludes that they must enjoy a large
income. The narrator tersely comments: 'Pero aquel Golfín era
un poco inocente en cosas del mundo, y como había pasado la
mayor parte de su vida en el extranjero, conocía mal nuestras
costumbres y esta especialidad del vivir madrileño, que en otra
parte se llamarían *misterios,* pero que aquí no son misterios
para nadie' (XXXIII, 1647). Teodoro's remarks of encourage-
ment to Francisco before his treatment begins are loaded with
an irony that the surgeon, unable to penetrate the family mys-
teries, does not appreciate: '[dijo] "Usted verá lo que nunca
ha visto", queriendo ponderar así la plenitud de la facultad
preciosa que estimamos sobre todas las demás de nuestro
cuerpo' (XXX, 1643). Even on the physical level intended by
Golfín, this prediction will not prove accurate, for the Revolution (which fulfils the prophecy in another, unintended, sense)
will once more upset Francisco's physical vision.

   The selection of Francisco's loss of sight as his main fictional development has enabled Galdós to raise a number of
important considerations concerning the relative merits or disadvantages of physical vision, moral insight and wild fantasy.
Because the central episode deals with eyesight all other references to this physical quality, to the eyes themselves, take on
an important secondary meaning they would not otherwise
have. In the above examples of character behaviour (the analysis
of which will be completed in Chapter 8) the considerable number of allusions to sight and the power of physical vision is a
sign that this subject is of deliberate importance to Galdós in
the elaboration of his characters and the drawing of his theme.
This opinion is substantiated to some extent by Galdós's occasional puns on words of optical significance: Rosalía muses at
the end: '¿A quién volver los ojos? Los de Bringas veían'
(XLI, 1664). Great play is made with the popular expression
'ojo de la cara' which normally means 'a great deal of money'.
Milagros uses the phrase with this meaning when she refers
to the high cost of dresses (XI, 1605). However, the literal
meaning is intended when Pez recalls how he was attacked in
San Sebastián by a titled lady for not getting customs clearance
on her fashion purchases: 'por poco me saca los ojos' (XXXVI,
1654). The combined, double layer of literal and metaphorical

meaning (the latter slightly adapted) is aptly applied to the costs of Golfín's treatment. Francisco moans: 'Él me curará los de la cara, pero me sacará un ojo del bolsillo' (XXXII, 1646; see also XX, 1623). Since for Francisco vision is a purely physical activity that he prizes above all others, and thrift is his dominating passion, the play on words captures pithily this inversion of values. Similar comic effects are produced by the frequent use of the metaphorical 'veremos' at important junctures: Pez employs the word to keep Rosalía on tenterhooks after their adultery (XLIV, 1669), or to suggest to Francisco that Paquito will be promoted (XXVIII, 1639). The same word is pronounced by Rosalía as she looks forward to the Revolution (XLVIII, 1679) or when she gives Milagros hope of a loan (XXIV, 1631). The rhetoric of vision is used by the characters, not to focus on the meaning of reality, but to encourage wild dreams or hopes of recovery of the physical faculty.

La de Bringas is indeed a novel about perspective and vision, their advantages and disadvantages. But what first of all appears to be a discussion centred exclusively on the physical faculty (in the description of the hair-picture and Francisco's illness) soon becomes enlarged, as is shown by the careful emphasis on the double meanings of optical terms, to include the question of another type of vision, that of the mind: good, if it is moral insight; bad, if it is unchecked imagination. Thus *La de Bringas* becomes a novel about the correct perception of reality, both physical and spiritual, seeing all of life in the right perspective (*47*, p. 8). But the question of perspective — now in the literary sense — had of course preceded *La de Bringas*'s composition. The sequel to *El doctor Centeno* and *Tormento* had been eagerly awaited by Galdós's friends and critics. Galdós was obliged to meet these expectations, but he did so in an appropriately perplexing fashion.

3. 'La de Bringas' and 'Tormento'

WHATEVER the validity of Orlando's contention that *La de Bringas* should have been tacked on to *Tormento* (26, pp. 444-5), it does show that these two novels have a closer association than that normally provided by a common theme or group of characters. Shoemaker (45, p. 424) reckons that the name given Refugio proves that Galdós had already planned the famous scene in *La de Bringas*. Greater weight to this theory is provided by the picture of Francisco Bringas at the beginning of *Tormento* where he is portrayed as a healthy, robust individual in 1867. However, a forward view of the man as he appears to the narrator in 1884 is added: 'Los que le tratamos entonces, apenas le reconocemos hoy cuando en la calle se nos aparece, dando el brazo a un criado, arrastrando los pies, hecho una curva, con media cara dentro de una bufanda, casi sin vista, tembloroso, baboso, y tan torpe de palabra como de andadura' (II, 1474). This description tallies remarkably well with our final view of Francisco in *La de Bringas,* but has no counterpart in *Tormento.* Ricard *(32)* has also demonstrated how in the characterization of Rosalía in *La de Bringas* Galdós has expanded many points that were minor or only partially developed in the preceding novel, a natural enough process when a secondary character in one novel becomes the protagonist of the sequel. However, this technique is also applied to microscopic details of fact: Francisco's skill with hair in *La de Bringas* is expanded from a passing comment made by Rosalía to Amparo in *Tormento:* 'Luego vas a la peluquería, y me traes el *crêpé* y el pelo, que Bringas me hace los añadidos [hair-pieces], y también hará uno para ti' (X, 1496). Similarly, Pez's securing of a Civil Service position for Paquito Bringas is the fulfilment of a promise made in *Tormento* (VI, 1488). For those who had not read the first novel, these correspondences of varying degrees would naturally lack interest, but for the regular reader, whose number Galdós was always anxious to increase, they offered a source of secret satisfaction and extra meaning, if recognized. The high number of such correspondences, possibly unequalled in any other pair of novels by Galdós (*32*, p. 49), forces comparisons to be made between the two novels, yet because these reverberations are so perplexing and baffling even for the regular Galdós reader, as we shall see in the chapter on characterization, Galdós is able to attract even more attention to the peculiar nature of *La de Bringas*.

A similarly perplexing effect is produced by the employ-ment of reappearing characters from other novels prior to *Tormento*. This common literary device which Galdós had learnt early from Balzac naturally validates the fictional world of *La de Bringas* and unifies it with that of its predecessors. However, the list of characters and novels is surprisingly large:

> *Marianela:* Celipín, Golfín.
> *Gloria:* Gloria, Juan de Lantigua and Serafinita, Rafael del Horro.
> *La familia de León Roch:* Milagros and family, Federico Cimarra, Pilar San Salomó, Francisco Cucúrbitas, el marqués de Fúcar, Onésimo.
> *La desheredada:* Sánchez Botín, the Pez family, the Aran-sis family, Muñoz y Nones, Onésimo.
> *El amigo Manso:* Máximo Manso, Cándida, Irene, Fede-rico Cimarra and Milagros.
> *El doctor Centeno:* Celipín, de la Caña family, Muñoz y Nones.
> *Episodios nacionales* (second series): Juan de Pipaón.

Some critics (*16*, pp. 125-8; *26*) have reacted, perhaps under-standably, with bewilderment and irritation; nevertheless, this is not the normal reaction to the employment of this device.[13] In the first instance, most of these characters reappear towards the beginning (in Chapter VII) at that important moment in any novel when the introductory material is giving way to the plot proper; not quite the moment for a sudden and quick

---

[13] Anthony R. Pugh, *Balzac's Recurring Characters* (Toronto: University of Toronto Press, 1974), p. 82.

reminder of the plots of a large number of other novels.
Secondly, more confusion is generated by the number of novels
recalled and the fact that some of the characters appear in
more than one of these. Thirdly, the nature of these reappear-
ances varies: in most cases Galdós lets the name speak for
itself, the reader having to jog his own memory. In other cases
he can be semi-explicit as when he alludes to the previous appearance of Milagros ('La belleza de Milagros no había llegado
aún al ocaso en que se nos aparece en la triste historia de su
yerno [i.e., León Roch]' (IX, 1601), or that of Carolina Pez:
'La señora de Pez, por nombre Carolina, prima de los Lanti-
guas (aunque equivocadamente, se ha dicho en otra historia
[i.e., *La desheredada*] que descendía del frondoso árbol pipaó-
nico)' (XIII, 1608). This last example shows the extent to which
Galdós was consciously using the device: he clearly felt that
he could change even such a minor detail of genealogy established in a preceding novel. Fourthly, these reappearing characters are taken from novels published earlier but whose action
occurs at a time later than that of *La de Bringas*. The result
is that we now see some old friends in new guises: adults are
now presented as children (Gloria, Irene and María Egipcíaca).
In the cases of Cándida and Milagros this disruption of narrative chronology is clearly indicated: 'A esto llamaba Máximo
Manso *la segunda manera de doña Cándida,* y debo hacer
constar que aún hubo una *tercera manera* mucho más lasti-
mosa' (XXI, 1624; see also V, 1594; VI, 1595).

The only exception to this chronological juggling is *Marianela,* written in 1878 and relating events that occurred in the
1860s, a fact deducible only from the imprecise date on Marianela's tombstone. This may be pure coincidence, but *Marianela*'s relationship with *La de Bringas,* forged by the reappearance
of Golfín, is especially significant. In a less subtle manner,
Marianela had presented the same opposition between the relative values of physical eyesight and moral insight that is the
core of *La de Bringas*'s argument. Moreover, if the events of
Marianela take place before those of *La de Bringas* (that Golfín
returned to Spain after his 1868 summer trip to Germany and
spent the following months in Socartes is less probable), then
Golfín has not absorbed the spiritual lesson presented earlier

by Marianela's death: 'No sé —replicó Teodoro, inquieto, confundido, aterrado, contemplando aquel libro humano de caracteres obscuros, en los cuales la vista científica no podía descifrar la leyenda misteriosa de la muerte y la vida' (XXI, 773). A structural parallel also strengthens this connection: in the first chapter of *Marianela* Teodoro Golfín loses his way in the Socartes forest and has to be led to the village by blind Pablo and Marianela. In the first scene proper of *La de Bringas,* after the introduction of the hair-picture, the narrator and Pez are both confident of finding their way through the Palace labyrinth (the use of the phrase 'adelante, adelante siempre seguíamos', IV, 1592 is a verbal parallel), but are compelled to accept the guidance of the otherwise unreliable Cándida.

True to its perplexing nature, *La de Bringas* also points forward to future novels as well as referring back to previous Galdós best-sellers. Some critics have maintained that Galdós was intending to write a sequel to *La de Bringas* (*14*, p. 119; *28*, p. 599). Some final comments by the narrator lend credence to this possibility, but again Galdós may be playing his game of ambiguous perspectives with the reader: 'Cómo se las compondría para este fin es cosa que no cae dentro de este relato. Las nuevas trazas de esta señora no están aún en nuestro tintero' (L, 1683). Really Galdós is suggesting that the position of *La de Bringas* in the corpus of his works can be viewed on many levels: it can be seen as an independent, self-contained volume, or closely related to its immediate predecessor in the sub-series, *Tormento,* or finally, it can be compared to earlier novels or may anticipate future ones. The more extensive the scope of relationships, the denser and richer the interpretation of *La de Bringas.* By deliberately presenting the nature of these relationships in an unusual and mystifying way Galdós focusses attention on the theme that *La de Bringas* shares with the other novels: the inability of people to correctly perceive the reality of life. In so doing, he has gone beyond the narrow expectations of those readers who might have merely wanted to read of new adventures befalling old characters. But also Galdós's presentation of the major setting in this novel is much better than in previous novels and must have surpassed the readers' expectations.

4. Setting

THE selection of the servants' quarters in the Madrid Royal Palace has often been praised for its originality (*16*, pp. 133, 278; *28*, p. 601; *33*, p. 62). Perhaps even more noteworthy is the manner in which Galdós is able to suggest through the accumulation of physical detail in his description the dominating impression of chaos, repugnance, beneath the building's smooth exterior:

> Viendo por fuera la correcta mole del alcázar, *no se comprenden* las irregularidades de aquel pueblo fabricado en sus pisos altos. Es que durante un siglo no se ha hecho allí más que modificar a troche y moche la distribución primitiva, tapiando por aquí, abriendo por allá, condenando escaleras, ensanchando unas habitaciones a costa de otras, convirtiendo la calle en vivienda y la vivienda en calle, agujereando paredes y cerrando huecos. Hay escaleras que empiezan y no acaban; vestíbulos o plazoletas en que se ven blanqueadas techumbres que fueron de habitaciones inferiores. Hay palomares donde antes hubo salones, y salas que un tiempo fueron caja de una gallarda escalera. Las de caracol se encuentran en varios puntos, sin que se sepa a dónde van a parar, y puertas tabicadas, huecos con alambrera, tras los cuales no se ve más que soledad, polvo y tinieblas ... aquel laberíntico pueblo *formado de recovecos, burladeros y sorpresas, caprichos de la arquitectura y mofa de la simetría.* (my italics; IV, 1592)

This process of constant architectural modification, still operative according to Cándida, produces an absurd, futile use of space. Above all it is the result of the caprice or fantasy of the Palace inhabitants whose inability to see reality from the proper perspective is the novel's major theme. In this way, Galdós transforms a routine background description into a vivid visual cipher of the novel's meaning. [14]

Upon this base of a confusing physical impression, Galdós then constructs an equally confusing series of associated images. The first analogy is with the hair-picture. The description of the Chapel cupola ('En efecto, grandes formas piramidales forradas de plomo nos indicaban las grandes techumbres en cuya superficie inferior hacen volatines los angelones de Bayeu', IV, 1592) recalls the 'piramidal escalinata, zócalos grecorromanos, y luego machones y paramentos ojivales, con pináculos, gárgolas y doseletes' (I, 1587) of the tomb in the hair-picture. The reference to the Palace as a 'fabricada montaña' (IV, 1592) is another visual and verbal parallel.

The servants' quarters are then likened to a tunnel or labyrinth in which the appropriately-named Pez resembles a character from a Jules Verne novel (IV, 1592) and the Palace guard 'un cancerbero con sombrero de tres picos' (III, 1591). And yet this imagined subterranean perspective jars with the upward physical trajectory of the two visitors. The contradictory juxtaposition of opposing ideas continues with the description of these quarters as a crown upon the head of the Monarchs: 'es una real república que los monarcas se han puesto por corona, y engarzadas en su inmenso círculo, guarda muestras diversas de toda clase de personas' (III, 1591). Though the servants are nominally the subjects of the Monarch, they will soon become the masters because of the September Revolution; for the moment they manipulate the Monarchs; thus the image, whose paradox is increased by the murky light, rather than the glow, of this particular crown, eventually appears justified *(47)*. The references to crown and republic suggest that these Palace quarters are also a microcosm of Spanish society, found outside the Palace in the city of Madrid. Moreover, the quarters are repeatedly described as a city (III, IV, 1591; V, 1594-5; VI, 1595). The peripatetic Cándida returns from her daily visits

---

[14] Ángel Fernández de los Ríos, *Guía de Madrid, manual del madrileño y del forastero* (Madrid: Ilustración Española y Americana, 1876), pp. 236-7, notes the number of times the plans for the principal staircase of the Palace were changed for no apparent reason.

PLAN I: ROYAL APARTMENTS

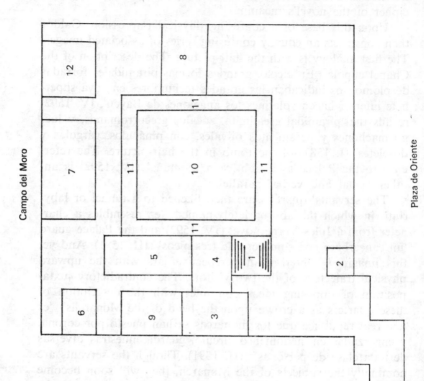

1 Escalera principal
2 Salón de Armas
3 Salón del Trono (also called Salón de Embajadores)
4 Salón de Guardias (also called El Camón)
5 Salón de Columnas
6 Salón de Gasparini
7 Comedor de Gala
8 Capilla Real
9 La Saleta
10 Patio central
11 La Terraza
12 Biblioteca Real

PLAN II: THE BRINGAS APARTMENT

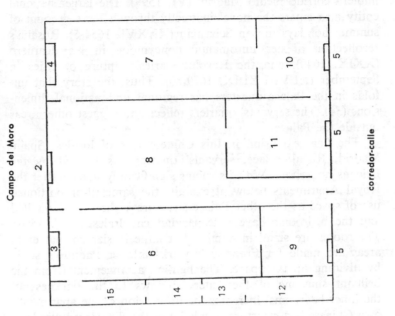

1 Puerta de entrada
2 Retrato de Juan de Pipaón
3 Biblioteca de Paquito
4 Despacho de Francisco
5 Claraboyas
6 Gabinete de la izquierda (*La Saleta*)
7 Gabinete de la derecha (*Gasparini*)
8 La sala (*Salón de Embajadores*)

9 Alcoba de la izquierda=comedor (*Salón de Columnas*)
10 Alcoba matrimonial (*Gasparini*)
11 Alcoba de la sala = guardarropa, cuarto de labor de Rosalía (*el Camón*)
12 Cocina
13 Pieza interior donde se plancha (*la Furriela*)
14-15 Dos piezas interiores donde dormían los hijos

to friends in other parts of the Palace 'tan rendida como si hubiera corrido medio Madrid' (VI, 1596). The larger national entity also enters the novel indirectly through Pez's account of summer holidays in San Sebastián (XXXVI, 1654-5), Rosalía's recollection of her unromantic honeymoon in Navalcarnero (XXIX, 1640), and the Revolutionaries' capture of cities in September (XLVIII-XLIX, 1679-80). Thus, the story that unfolds in the Palace quarters has regional and national dimensions (*34*). The servants' quarters reflect and suggest other areas outside the Palace.

The final extension in this Chinese box of locales (Spain, Madrid, Royal Palace, servants' quarters) is formed by the Bringas household. With its rooms significantly named after the Royal Apartments below, it exhibits the same ill-proportioned use of space as the other Palace structures: the roof is vaulted and the bedrooms have a 'capacidad catedralesca' (V, 1594). The rooms are small in number but large in size so that extra areas are made for Francisco's work-table or Paquito's study by dividing up the space. The lighting arrangement (from the brilliant sunshine of the outer windows to the darkness of the inner bedrooms) increases the impression of the apartment's own Chinese-box structure, symbolic of the disordered minds of its inhabitants. This room plan is also used to good effect in the plot: Francisco works away on one side of the house (4 on Plan II) and Rosalía on the other (11). Even after Francisco's removal to a darker area of the house when he loses his sight, physical space is cleverly used by Rosalía to avoid embarrassing explanations to her husband, as she returns money to Torres (XXI, 1624) or changes her new peignoir. However, during Francisco's relapse, Rosalía's spiritual rapprochement to her husband is reflected spatially: she stays close beside Francisco tending to his needs and locks her clothes in the *Camón* (XXXI, 1644). The apartment's location within the Palace (on the west side facing the Campo del Moro) also contributes to the plot development: because of the evening heat inside Francisco urges Rosalía to accompany Pez on the terrace and thus helps to bring the two future adulterers closer together. Thus once more we can see how Galdós is not content to record just the physical dimensions of his setting. The latter is skilfully integrated into the plot and theme of his novel, contributing to the overall effect.

The Royal Palace remains the principal setting for most of the novel. [15] When in the first two-thirds of the novel Galdós wishes to avoid the monotony of the same setting, he introduces other locations which continue the basic style and nature of the Palace so that these secondary locales may be considered extensions of the latter. This association is strengthened by the fact that these alternative places are frequented exclusively by the Palace society. For example, we are taken (through Rosalía's recollections, XIV) to Milagros's disordered house in the Calle de Atocha. Other substitute locales include Sobrino Hermanos and the Royal Enclosure of the Retiro Park (Lo Reservado) where the Bringas children clamber up 'las espirales de la Montaña artificial, que es, en verdad, el colmo del artificio. Todos aquellos regios caprichos así como La Casa de Fieras, declaran la época de Fernando VII, que, si en política fue brutalidad, en artes, fue tontería pura' (XVI, 1613). Details in this description such as 'caprichos, espirales, montaña' and the mention of Fernando VII refer us not only to the Palace structure but also to the hair-picture.

However, in the last third of the novel (really from Chapter XXXVII to the end) the descriptions of the Palace and its extensions diminish and when they do occur, are now characterized by a blatant breakdown of order: the lesser servants pull their tertulia chairs onto the terrace where formerly Pez and Rosalía had paraded pretentiously, or hold wild all-night parties on the third floor, to the shocked indignation of Cándida (XXXVIII, 1658). More scenes now take place outside the Royal compound. Plot developments determine to some extent this change of setting: with all her friends away in the North, Rosalía has nothing else to do but wander around the shops or seek company in the Prado tertulias. None the less, Galdós's decision to present these places directly to the reader at this

---

[15] William R. Risley, 'Setting in the Galdós Novel, 1881-1885', *HR*, XLVI (1978), 23-40 (at p. 31), points out that of the novels Galdós wrote between 1881 and 1887 *La de Bringas* contains the highest proportion of settings.

point (the summer months of 1868) is especially appropriate in that the descriptions, although very realistic, maintain the principal features of the earlier Palace and hair-work pictures: the bizarre, incongruent mixture of pleasant, attractive appearances and an underlying repugnant reality. The poetic names of the Manzanares swimming pools (Los Jerónimos, los Cipreses, el Arco Iris, La Esmeralda and El Andaluz) do not match the dirty reality of their facilities: 'También Paquito se arrojaba, intrépido, a las ondas de aquellos pequeños mares sucios, metidos entre esteras, y nadaba que era un primor, en pie sobre el fondo' (XXXVIII, 1658). In the streets of Madrid, repugnance and attractiveness alternate with terrifying effects on Rosalía:

Cuando [Rosalía] iba a dar una vueltecita por las tiendas, la mortificaban los olores que por diversas puertas salían en las calles más populosas, olor de humanidad y de guisotes. Las rejas de los sótanos despedían en algunos sitios una onda de frescura que la convidaba a detenerse; mas en aquellos sótanos donde había cocinas, el vaho era tan repugnante que la empujaba hacia el arroyo. Veía con delicia las mangas de riego sintiendo ganas de recibir la ducha en sus propias carnes; pero luego se desprendía del suelo un vapor asfixiante, mezclado de emanaciones nada balsámicas, que la obligaba a avivar el paso. Los perros bebían en los charcos sucios formados por los chorros de riego, y después refugiábanse a la sombra, como los vendedores ambulantes. (XXXVIII, 1659-60) [16]

To Rosalía Madrid does not seem like Madrid but 'un lugarón poblado de la gente más zafia y puerca del mundo... creía hallarse en un pueblo de moros, según la idea que tenía de las ciudades africanas' (XXXVIII, 1659). This popular reality which Rosalía finds so distasteful is present, nevertheless, all

[16] Galdós's contemporary description of the 1868 Madrid summer appears in his articles for *La Nación* on May 31 and June 7; see William H. Shoemaker, *Los artículos de Galdós en 'La Nación' 1865-1866, 1868* (Madrid: Ínsula, 1972), pp. 533-40.

the time on the third floor of the Palace, as Pez and the narrator had observed (IV, 1592). Torquemada's house in the Travesía de Moriana contains a strange assortment of luxurious objects pawned by Palace servants like Milagros and Bringas (XLI, 1666) whilst Refugio's apartment with clothes strewn everywhere estrafalaria mezcla de cosas buenas y malas', XLV, 1672) is ('Nunca había visto [Rosalía] desbarajuste semejante ni tan surrounded by very respectable neighbours: religious and clothes shops. In the constant interaction between Madrid and the Royal Palace (*33*, p. 66), Galdós's manipulation of locales at different times in the book has exposed the discordant mixture that is common to both entities, except that the proportions of external gloss, inner chaos, are inverted.

That this mixture of order and chaos in physical structures does not determine but rather is determined by a corresponding mixture of mental or spiritual order and chaos is an important argument against the supposed Naturalism of the novel (see my Introduction). Of course, the impressive surroundings of the Palace do exert some effect on the behaviour of the characters: as Pez and Rosalía stroll on the terrace 'el paseo por sitio monumental *halagaba la fantasía* de la dama, trayéndole reminiscencias de aquellos fondos arquitectónicos que Rubens, Veronés, Vanloo y otros pintores ponen en sus cuadros, con lo que magnifican las figuras y les dan un aire muy aristocrático. Pez y Rosalía *se suponían destacados elegantemente sobre* aquel fondo de balaustradas, molduras, archivoltas y jarrones, suposición que, *sin pensarlo, los compelía a armonizar su apostura y aun su paso con la majestad de la escena*' (my italics; XII, 1606). However, the Bringas's style of living is already well established before they move into the Palace. In *Tormento* the Bringas's ground-floor apartment in the Costanilla de los Ángeles is also described as a labyrinth (of which they are proud) (III, 1479). So, then, is Agustín's luxurious, modern mansion (XXXIV, 1570). Rosalía's sewing-room is already cluttered with material (V, 1483) and the living room is also likened to the Royal chamber, Gasparini (III, 1478). Evidently the move to the Palace did not change the family's disordered domestic habits, nor did it foment them. Labyrinthine structures suited these characters, whether they were to be found within or

without the Royal Palace. Whatever the merits of Palley's view
that the Palace is another character in the novel (*40*, p. 340),
there can be no doubt that Galdós succeeds in transforming the
heavily detailed photographs of his physical settings into vivid
emblems of the novel's major theme. They are further integrated into the fabric of the novel by the careful structure Galdós
gives his material.

5. Structure

THE extended series of locale descriptions has often been cited as evidence that *La de Bringas* is a poorly constructed novel with little plot development (*6*, p. 81; *12*, pp. 61-2; *26*, p. 445). Such a view fails to take into account that *La de Bringas* is not a typical adventure novel (ridiculed in *Tormento* by Ido del Sagrario's pot-boilers) where background description is a quick, convenient springboard from which to launch the dramatic action. In *La de Bringas,* on the other hand, description of settings and plot development are constantly oscillating in order to elucidate the moral theme in which Galdós is vitally interested. The description of Refugio's apartment (XLV, 1672) is a good example. At this dramatic juncture in the novel, the detailed account might appear an unnecessary obstacle. Yet because it is used as part of the thematic development of the scene (Galdós presents it to Rosalía as a visual lesson of her own house's disorder) it cannot be dismissed as irrelevant.

The structure of the novel's chapters can be summarized as follows:

> *Introduction*: (I-X): description of the hair-picture, the Palace quarters, the Bringas house and their friends; the Maundy Thursday ceremony; beginning of Rosalía's close friendship with Milagros.
>
> *Part I* (X-XIX): Rosalía's purchase of the shawl; problems in repaying the loan to Torres; her friendship with Pez; Francisco's attack of blindness.
>
> *Part II* (XX-XXXI): Francisco's partial recovery, then relapse and rapprochement with Rosalía, who pawns the candelabra; her discovery of Francisco's savings.
>
> *Part III* (XXXII-XLIV): Francisco regains sight; Rosalía's difficulties in repaying Torquemada; her unrewarded adultery with Pez.

Conclusion (XLV-L): Refugio gives Rosalía the money she needs. With the triumph of the September Revolution, the Bringas family leaves the Palace.

This schema with its climaxes is produced by the constant intertwining of four threads of action: political developments; Francisco's work on the hair-picture and its consequences; Rosalía's affair with Pez; and her friendship with Milagros.

The political strand is used chiefly to begin and end the novel. The move of the Bringas family to the Royal Palace which brings Rosalía and Milagros into a fatally closer contact is the result of a political promotion for Francisco. The family's sad departure from the Palace and Francisco's continued ignorance of his wife's spending is ensured by the outbreak of the September Revolution. Apart from one moment when González Bravo's offer of a provincial governorship to Francisco might have solved Rosalía's economic difficulties and brought an end to the story (XV, 1612), the dramatic interest after the Introduction derives from the alternative interweaving of the other three strands in response to the initial situation: Rosalía's inability to pay for the shawl in cash. The paradox is that Francisco's attack of blindness and his subsequent physical condition, far from increasing this initial problem of Rosalía's as they first appear to do, lead to its ultimate solution: in the short term, she is able to secure loans from Torres and Torquemada, or pawn valuable objects; in the long term, she receives the large sum of cash from Refugio and is able to carry on her profitable series of seductions; all without the knowledge of Francisco. Refugio's resumption of relations with the Bringas family is also prompted by Francisco's sudden illness: the Caballeros in Bordeaux send her to the Palace to enquire after his condition. Moreover, the two people whom Rosalía sincerely relies upon to extricate her from her financial difficulties, Pez and Milagros, are surprisingly unhelpful. Thus the novel's basic theme and texture — a confusing perspectivism — is well illustrated in the working out of the four threads of action.

In their constant interaction, Galdós is also able to reproduce this surprising perspectivism. The outbreak of the Revolution, rumoured to be imminent at the beginning of the novel, appears to recede in the middle chapters with the banishment of the Generals to the Canary Islands, only to materialize, surprisingly, at the end. We have already noted the ups and downs of Francisco's blindness (p. 27). Pez's amorous advances towards Rosalía grow in intensity, are then rebuffed, but eventually (and to his great surprise) are rewarded without any financial cost, after his summer holidays away from Madrid. In her desperate search for money, Milagros suggests that Francisco's savings should be given to her (XVIII, 1618). Francisco's initial attack of blindness and her own securing of a short-term loan interrupt this request which, however, she renews with even greater intensity a week later (XXIII, 1629). A further, even stronger, request is to no avail (XXX, 1641); Rosalía's eventual donation, coming as a great surprise, is the result of the sudden intervention of another strand: Rosalía's discovery of Francisco's savings. This baffling pattern of surprise developments, summed up and compressed in the climactic scene between Rosalía and Refugio, is, however, not so contradictory or baffling as it first appears. The sudden developments that change the novel's direction producing the respective climaxes of Parts I-III of our schema (Francisco's blindness; Rosalía's discovery of his treasure; her adultery with Pez; the outbreak of the Revolution) are, despite the suddenness of their presentation, entirely predictable from the data previously given: Francisco had been warned by friends, even by his children, that he will go blind if he continues with his hair-work; it has been very clear that Rosalía is greatly attracted to Pez, so her adultery is not altogether unexpected; there has been no indication that the anti-Government plotting has stopped even though the Generals have been imprisoned, and there is no doubt that Francisco has amassed some savings.

To widen this pattern of confusing perspectives, Galdós also employs a device which might be termed 'ironic reprise': the comparatively close repetition of one scene by an inverted parallel, with consequent transfers of ironic meaning (*38*, p. 58). [17] The distorted reproductions of Palace and domestic scenes

---

[17] Monroe Z. Hafter, 'Ironic Reprise in Galdós' Novels', *Publications of the Modern Language Association of America*, LXXXVI (1961),

in Isabelita's nightmares (VIII, 1600; XXXIV, 1650-1) are the most obvious of several examples that can be cited. Francisco's ecstatic vision of the completed hair-picture (II, 1589), whose actual gaudy condition has already been given to the reader, receives its own ironic reprise later when Francisco promises to make Rosalía a wardrobe on his full recovery of sight: "'Vamos bien, bien. Vea yo, y verán todos mis obras" era lo que, sin cesar, decía' (XXV, 1633). His conviction that it will be as popular a tourist attraction as the Palace stables; his use of old Palace wood and space for the job; the mention of other royal residences; the designation of Francisco as an artist; the use of Cándida's furniture as models; these are all reminders of the hair-picture (and the Palace quarters). The difference, of course, is that now Francisco is going to construct something of mammoth, not minuscule, proportions: 'un panteón para la ropa' (XXV, 1633). His excited mind is still thinking in absurdly exaggerated terms.

Pez's unconscious self-criticism when describing to Rosalía his wife's complaints (XIII, 1609) is mirrored in the next chapter by Rosalía's equally unconscious self-indictment when describing the weakness of Milagros for clothes-buying, and her attendant domestic problems (XIV, 1609-11). In an extended ironic inversion, the marqués de Tellería's reported discovery of Milagros's secret purchases is paralleled by Francisco's real discovery of Rosalía's own secret purchases (XV, 1611).

Other examples of structural 'ironic reprise' are less developed, though none the less frequent, in the novel. During their Retiro promenades, Rosalía sings Francisco's praises to Pez (XVI, 1614), yet alone in her house afterwards she vents very different feelings — now of scorn for his penny-pinching ways (XVII, 1615; see also XXIX, 1640). Cándida's surprise announcement that she has money to invest (a lie and really the prelude to a request for money, XVIII-XIX, 1618-19) is made to the incredulous Rosalía and Milagros just after the latter

---

233-9, examines the use of this technique in Galdós's novels in terms only of the characterization. In *La de Bringas* Galdós applies the technique to the novel's structure and language as well.

has tried to use the investment argument to secure some of Francisco's savings. Pez's realistic account of summer holidays in the North prefaces Milagros's detailed relation of her preparations for the vacation (XXXVII, 1656-7). In an attempt to persuade Golfín to lower his charges, Francisco states that he has been put on half-pay (XXXII, 1647). Two chapters later the 'burlas' become 'veras' when Vargas reports the decision of the Intendente to this effect. This pattern of ironic reverberations from one scene to another allows Galdós to depart from a rigidly monolinear plot progression. At the same time, however, it does help to illustrate, through the apparent contradiction of progressive and regressive developments, the confusing perspectives of meaning presented by *La de Bringas*.

A very similar effect is achieved by the adroit manipulation of temporal references whose function as seen by Sánchez (*44*) was only to indicate, through greater or lesser precision, the corresponding increase or decrease in the urgency of Rosalía's loan repayments. First it must be established that Galdós's extreme attention to chronological detail, whilst giving an impression of a faithful reproduction of the 1868 calendar, never plots days against the actual historical dates of that year. Secondly, the pattern of temporal references is more complex and varied than Sánchez's polarity of precision and imprecision might suggest. Galdós can be precise about the actual hour in which an event occurred as when he times Rosalía's visit to Refugio; 'El tiempo apremiaba: ya había dado la una' (XLV, 1673). Alternatively, he can be extremely vague as when he records Refugio's first visit to the Bringas's house: 'por aquellos días' (XXVI, 1635). More interestingly, at times he substitutes well-known saints' days for dates (XXXIV, 1649; XXXIII, 1628; XXXIX, 1660). However, it is in the chronological sequence of events that Galdós can at times present some perplexing incongruities, as the introductory chapters show. Initial work on the hair-picture takes place in February and March of 1868 (III, 1590); we are then told that the Bringas family moved into the Palace in February (III, 1591). On the other hand, the date of the narrator's and Pez's first visit is not recorded (III, 1591). Instead, the narrator does specify the date

of 4 October 1868 (VI, 1595) (that is, a time which is reached
only at the end of the novel) when he sends Francisco some
bottles of wine and fowls for his birthday. Furthermore, the
reader is propelled to later years, beyond the novel's chronology
(if back in time in his own memory of Galdós's previously
published novels) by the case histories of Cándida, Milagros
and other friends of the Bringas family (VI-X). After this confusing mixture of temporal divisions, the story proper starts
with Rosalía's purchase of the shawl in April 1868 (XI, 1604).

The many references to González Bravo's banishment of
the Unión Liberal generals to the Canary Islands on 7 July
1868 offer another example of the care with which Galdós uses
time to produce perplexing effects on the reader. The first mention, by Francisco to Pez, presumably a rumour spread just
before or at the actual time of the banishment ('¿Qué hay de
destierro de generales?', XII, 1607) is included in an example
of Pez's rhetorical style in the general character description of
the bureaucrat. However, this description is given at a time in
the plot when other events are occurring much earlier, in April.
The second reference to the banishment is encased in the cryptic
exchange of remarks between Cándida and Francisco that pre-
ludes the latter's loss of vision on June 13: '*Revolución . . . Generales . . . Canarias . . . Montpensier*' (XIX, 1621). The impression given is that the Generals have now been sent to the
Canaries. In the next allusion (XXVII, 1637), during Tula's
soporific tertulia, their arrival in the Canary Islands is given
as a fact. Nevertheless, this enigmatic scene is not given a precise dating. The nearest chronological references — 'por aquellos
días' (XXIV, 1631; XXVI, 1635) — are singularly unhelpful.
The nearest precise reference is 26 June when Milagros faints
and sobs on Rosalía's shoulder during an attempt to elicit
financial support (XXIII, 1629). Indeed, the next precise date
after Tula's party is that of the Generals' exile itself (XXIX,
1641), although the mysterious overlap of scenes between Chapters XXVII and XXVIII suggests at first no change of day. As
if revelling in his chronological game with the reader, Galdós
now dutifully recalls in full detail the episode of the Generals'
imprisonment and probable exile: 'dicen que los mandarán a

Canarias' (**XXX**, 1642). Considering Francisco's earlier conversation with Pez on the subject and Rosalía's presence at Tula's party, their respective reactions of delighted surprise ('¿A Canarias? ¡A los quintos infiernos! — exclamó la Pipaón con júbilo'; '¿Conque a la sombra? ¡Hombre más bravo que ese presidente del Consejo…!') are baffling. Galdós knew very well the date of this important political event but his chronological presentation of it within the narrative is deliberately fragmented and disordered. [18]

In her nightmarish recollection of the Maundy Thursday ceremonies, Isabelita sees the Palace servants shouting madly: 'Ya es la hora' (**VIII**, 1600). Time, present and future, is of vital concern to these Palace inmates, but the irony is that they do not realize that time, in the form of the Revolution, is their greatest enemy: their world of social pretence is shortly to end or, true to the novel's perspectivism, will appear to end. Rosalía's story of temptation, like that of Milagros and Cándida, is limited by time: one Rosalía is giving way to another: '[Rosalía] admiraba a la Rosalía de la época anterior a los trampantojos que a la sazón la traían tan desconcertada' (**XLI**, 1665).

The net effect of this tightly-controlled and tightly-paced structure is that at times the novel appears to read like a drama; this is presumably what Montesinos had in mind when he referred to its French nature (*16*, p. 151). This impression is reinforced not only by the famous dramatic confrontation between Rosalía and Refugio but also by Galdós's occasional use of a theatrical format to present conversation. The most developed passage is to be found in our first glimpse of Rosalía and Milagros when they are discussing the latest fashions (**X**, 1602-3). The clear purpose of this device, besides creating a theatrical atmosphere, is to suggest the exaggerated behaviour and language, or artificiality, of the characters, indeed that their lives are acted out in the exaggerated outline of melodrama. [19]

---

[18] For Galdós's equally subtle play with temporal references in *Torquemada en la hoguera*, see Nicholas G. Round, 'Time and Torquemada: Three Notes on Galdosian Chronology', *AG*, **VI** (1971), 79-97.

[19] This function is surprisingly omitted by Roberto G. Sánchez, *El teatro en la novela: Galdós y Clarín* (Madrid: Ínsula, 1974).

Now only an infrequent theatregoer (XIV, 1609), Rosalía is
often described as an actress studying a part when she deceives
Francisco (XV, 1611; XVI, 1613; XXIX, 1640; XXXIII, 1648;
XLVIII, 1679). Galdós's final comment on her story is indeed
couched in the language of the stage: 'Y es que tales ocasiones
[Rosalía's humiliation by Refugio], lances, dramas mansos, o
como quiera llamárselos, fueron los ensayos de aquella mudanza moral, y debieron de cogerla inexperta y como novicia'
(L, 1683). The Maundy Thursday ceremony (VIII, 1599) and
Milagros's sponsored mass (XVIII, 1617) are presented as
absurd religious farces, theatrical performances. The sunsets
that figure prominently at important moments (Francisco's loss
of sight; his first temporary recovery, XXVIII, 1639; Pez's
final offer of monetary aid to Rosalía, XXXII, 1646; see also
47) are a common aspect of nineteenth-century melodrama that
Galdós uses as a stage-lighting cipher to emphasize the artificiality of these scenes. [20] The Realist counterpoint to this Romantic symbol is, of course, the red gas-shades in the corridor-
tunnels of the Palace (IV, 1591). The melodramatic, rather than
the dramatic, label is thus not inappropriate to describe the
structure of *La de Bringas*: despite the apparently taut and
logical frame, strange repetitions of scenes, temporal displace-
ments and plot surprises unsettle the reader anxious to follow a
normal linear plot progression. The fine arts also provide
another fruitful departure point: *La de Bringas* can be compared to a set of social paintings or photographs.

---

[20] See Peter Brook, *The Melodramatic Imagination*: *Balzac, Henry
James, Melodrama, and the Mode of Excess* (New Haven: Yale University Press, 1976), p. 47.

6. Social pictures

As a picture-book of contemporary social habits (27) *La de Bringas*, like most so-called Realist or Naturalist novels, has an extrinsic value: it provides useful documentation on the occupations, pastimes and attitudes (financial, religious and sexual) of a certain segment of the Spanish bourgeoisie in 1868. None the less, its social focus also takes in — albeit briefly — aristocratic and working-class lifestyles, in the Court ceremonies and the street scenes, respectively. This social comprehensiveness is not accidental, for Galdós is anxious in this novel to show that all sectors of Spanish society are afflicted by the same shortcomings: the Palace society is, as we have seen, presented as a microcosm of the larger entity. Equally deliberate and co-ordinated is Galdós's integration of these apparently background social photographs into the complex pattern of shifting perspectives that is *La de Bringas's* peculiar texture: they become important illustrations of the novel's principal theme of reality concealed by deceptive appearances.

a) Fashions

As Rosalía's absorption in the world of female fashions provides the main matter of the novel, detailed passages of material description are frequent. One example will suffice: 'En casa de los Hijos de Rotondo me han dado unas 25 varas de *Bareges,* muy arregladito. Me ha dicho la de San Salomó que el *Bareges* se llevará mucho este verano. Francamente, los *Mozambiques* me apestan ya' (XVI, 1613; see also X, 1602-3; XI, 1605; XV, 1611-12; XVIII, 1617; XXI, 1625; XXIII, 1628-9; XXVI, 1635; XXXV, 1652; XLII, 1667; XLV, 1672). How accurate are these descriptions? Montesinos believes in their total reliability (*16*, p. 133). Galdós's attention to detail is certainly extraordinary. He could well have culled the information from contemporary newspaper reports, the same source he had used for an article on a recent society ball for *La Prensa* of Buenos Aires. [21] If so, then he could be accused of a chronological inaccuracy, for the design of the dresses given in *La de Bringas,* with emphasis on the bustle or 'pouf', corresponds to 1884 rather than 1868. [22] The reason for this chronological inaccuracy as well as for the degree of detail (unequalled in any other Galdós novel) could well be a desire to disorient the regular reader who is forced to wade through this detail or circumvent it as Orlando did (*26*). Whichever course is taken, these frequent passages of dress description are sufficient to make the reader pause in his reading. If they are historically inaccurate, then greater is the author's joke at the other's expense. Spread around Rosalía's room (XV, 1611) or Refugio's apartment (XLV, 1672), the collections of clothes form a physical labyrinth comparable to those of the Palace structures and the hair-picture. The unusually consistent intermingling of French and Spanish terms to describe these materials also produces a confusion for the reader which Galdós readily acknowledges and ironically tries to dispel with a suitable sartorial image: 'Los términos franceses que matizaban este coloquio se despegaban del tejido de nuestra lengua; pero aunque sea clavándolos con alfileres los he de sujetar para que el exótico idioma de los trapos no pierda su genialidad castiza' (X, 1602). [23]

Furthermore, in almost all of these passages the pieces of clothing described are in the process of being assembled into a dress or are being discussed in a conversation; they are never

[21] William H. Shoemaker, *Las cartas desconocidas de Galdós en 'La Prensa' de Buenos Aires* (Madrid: Cultura Hispánica, 1973), pp. 63-71 (at p. 68).

[22] See Phillis Cunnington, *Costumes of the Nineteenth Century* (Boston: Plays, 1970); Victoria and Albert Museum, *Costume Illustration: the Nineteenth Century,* introd. James Laver (London: His Majesty's Stationery Office, 1947); and Paul H. Nystrom, *Economics of Fashion* (New York: Ronald, 1928), pp. 280-9.

[23] R. Turner Wilcox, *The Dictionary of Costume* (New York: Scribner's, 1969) and Maurice Leloir, *Dictionnaire du costume et de ses accessoires des armes et des étoffes des origines à nos jours* (Paris: Grund, 1951), are useful reference books for these terms.

presented directly as a garment actually worn by the ladies. The only complete pictures (the children's description of the dresses at the Maundy Thursday ceremony and Francisco's glimpse of Rosalía's new peignoir) are appropriately distanced and blurred. Clothes manufacture in this pre-mass-production age is a protracted and gradual accumulation of different shapes and layers of cloth that are attached according to the design of a pattern, in much the same way that the hairs in Francisco's hair-picture are attached to a basic design, and, one might add, in the same way that the elements in this novel and my corresponding analysis in this Guide are interwoven. This is really the method Rosalía has always used: 'Comprando los avíos en la subida de Santa Cruz, empalmando pedazos, disimulando remiendos, obtenía un resultado satisfactorio con mucho trabajo y poco dinero' (X, 1604). What changes in *La de Bringas* is not this method of dress-making but rather the quantity and quality of material she now uses. Ensconced with Milagros or a servant in her *Camón,* Rosalía still juggles with small pieces of material as she laboriously assembles a dress.

This obsession with clothes is not confined to females in the novel. In an exceptionally full description, Pez is introduced as a model of sartorial elegance:

> Vestía este caballero casi casi como un figurín. Daba gozo ver su extraordinaria pulcritud. Su ropa tenía la virtud de no ajarse ni empolvarse nunca, y le caía sobre el cuerpo como pintada. Mañana y tarde, Pez vestía de la misma manera, con levita cerrada de paño, pantalón que parecía estrenado el mismo día y chistera reluciente, sin que ese esmero pareciese afectado ni revelara esfuerzo o molestia en él. Así como en los grandes estilistas la excesiva lima parece naturalidad fácil, en él la corrección era como un desgaire bien aprendido. (XII, 1607)

Clothes assume such importance in the lives of these characters, both male and female, because they publicize visibly to the world the economic or social status of their wearers: clothes in fact become the person, all interest centering on external appearances at the cost of any spiritual life or even of a good physical life: the principal reason for taking a holiday in San

Sebastián is to make clothes-buying trips to Biarritz. And as
Refugio acidly indicates (XLVI, 1675) and Milagros's dinner
party proves (XIV, 1610), many bourgeois starve in order to
buy clothes for public display. However, this is another illusion,
for the clothes are never paid for; as Francisco ironically indicates to Refugio: 'Aquí el lujo está en razón inversa del dinero
con que pagarlo' (XXVI, 1636).

b) *Money*

Montesinos *(16)* classified *La de Bringas* as one of Galdós's
'novelas de la locura crematística'. Both Varey *(46)* and Gullón
(14) regard the theme of money as one of the most important
in the novel. Certainly Galdós's attention to financial minutiae
and to their integration into the overall pattern of the novel's
complex perspectives is typically careful. Francisco's annual
salary of 30,000 reales (III, 1591), roughly halfway up the Civil
Service scale, between Pez's 50,000 (XVII, 1615) and a lower
Palace servant's 6,000 (XXXVIII, 1658), is not sufficient to
maintain a high level of living. Neither is Pez's. Refugio's comments to Rosalía are highly revealing of the economic con-
ditions of the time: 'Y aquí, salvo media docena, todos son
pobres. Facha, señora, y nada más que facha' (XLVI, 1675). In
the economic depression of 1868 *(1,* pp. 299-304; *3,* pp. 64-79)
real wealth in Spain is concentrated in the hands of a few
people, the only group Rosalía considers exploiting at the end
of the novel (XLVIII, 1679-80). Their use of what little capital
there is (for their own sexual gratification) can hardly be described as in the interests of the national economy. Even the
otherwise sober Agustín Caballero fails to put his money to
good use when, through Amparo, he finances Refugio's drapery
business. Likewise Golfín uses his substantial earnings to travel
the world, oblivious to the true nature of Spanish society. An
even smaller percentage of capitalists will either hoard their
substantial capital (like Francisco) or invest it for maximum
personal profit (like Torquemada).

The revelation of Francisco's immense capital of 23,700
reales (XXXI, 1644) in the appropriately false-bottomed box
also fits into the novel's pattern of mystifying, graduated per-

spectives. In *Tormento* the Bringas savings appear to be non-existent: 'Así y todo, expuesto anduvo el tesoro bringuístico a caer en el horroroso abismo de la insolvencia' (XXVII, 1548). Granted that Francisco's subsequent promotion and move to the Palace allow him to recover from this position, the figure of 23,700 reales seems an impossibly large sum to have amassed in the short space of a few months, unless Francisco had always deliberately concealed the true state of the family's finances, motivated by his passion for hoarding.

In the same way the ever-growing financial needs of Rosalía conform to the novel's graduated pattern: her initial debt occasioned by the purchase of the shawl amounts to 1,700 reales; five months later this debt has snowballed into the staggering figure of 5,000 reales. To fund her addiction, Rosalía is forced to rely upon a number of sources whose operations fittingly increase in scope and magnitude commensurate with the extent of Rosalía's needs. In view of the general tendency for customers of fashion shops not to pay their bills, the credit Rosalía, like Milagros, can obtain so readily at Sobrino Hermanos is surprising, to say the least. Her next source, Torres, is a minor broker who takes a small commission for lending out other people's money on the short term. An anonymous pawnbroker sends her cash through the intermediary, Cándida, for the earrings and candelabra. Another professional, Torquemada, now lends her money after she has signed a document specifying the interest and commission rates, a procedure that had been earlier ridiculed by Milagros's farcical written pledge to Rosalía to return Francisco's money at interest (XXXI-II, 1645). Rosalía's ultimate dependence on Refugio marks her initiation into the world of big-money support from national and international financiers, when money is now repaid not with interest but with sexual favours. The proliferation of Rosalía's debt has thus involved almost all branches of the Spanish financial system. [24]

---

[24] Jaime Vicens Vives, *Manual de historia económica de España*, 3rd ed. (Barcelona: Vicens-Vives, 1964), pp. 661-3, gives a brief picture of the contemporary banking situation.

Rosalía's monetary difficulties are also compounded by two other weaknesses: her willingness to lend money to Milagros, and her uncontrollable urge to buy more odds and ends of material for herself and the children just as she is slowly amassing enough money to make the repayment (XI, 1604; XI, 1606; XVIII, 1616; XXI, 1624; XXXIII, 1648). In fact, discounts for these two weaknesses are built into her future requests for funds (XXXIII, 1648). Milagros vividly sums up this method of financial management with an image that at once recalls the hair-picture and the Palace structure: 'Pero cuando se van acumulando las dificultades, cuando se prolonga mucho el sistema de abrir un hueco para tapar otro y prorrogar y aplazar, llega un día en que todo se va de través; es como un barco ya muy viejo y remendado que de repente se abre ..., ¡plum! ... y ... Al llegar a esto del barco averiado, el lenguaje de la pobre señora, más que lenguaje era un sollozo continuo ...' (XXIII, 1629).

Varey *(46)* has convincingly shown that Galdós used the contemporary economic theories of Adolphe Thiers to ridicule the attitude of his fictional counterpart, Francisco Bringas, towards money, wealth and work. With his negligible office work typical of the Civil Service, as shown by the example of Pez (XIII, 1609), and his hoarding of money, Francisco is a caricature of the French statesman who in his apologia for capitalism had emphasized the work ethic as the basis of individual as well as collective wealth, pointing out that reinvestment of earned wealth contributed to the greater prosperity of both individual and State. Thiers's theories are also distorted by Milagros and Rosalía when they ponder the potential returns on Francisco's invested savings:

> Don Francisco debe de tener mucho *parné* guardado, dinero improductivo, onza sobre onza, a estilo de paleto. ¡Qué atraso tan grande! Así está el país como está, porque el capital no circula, porque todo el metálico está en las arcas, sin beneficio para nadie, ni para el que lo posee. Don Francisco es de los que piensan que el dinero debe criar telarañas.

...Volvió la de Tellería a explanar su proposición, robusteciéndola con razones de gran peso (¡Oh! ¡El dinero de
manos muertas es la causa del atraso de La Nación!).
(XVIII, 1618)

The same argument is later used by Rosalía to justify her
seizure of Francisco's savings: 'Guardar dinero de aquel modo,
sin obtener de él ningún producto, ¿no era una tontería? ¡Si
al menos lo diera a interés o lo emplease en cualquiera de las
sociedades que reparten dividendos ...' (XXXI, 1644-5). Both
women want to put Francisco's money to some use, but it is
a singularly selfish and frivolous use: manufacture of these
kinds of dresses can hardly be considered an industry vital to
the growth of Spain's economy at this time. [25] This sort of trade
caters to the 'caprichos' of people like Rosalía (XXXVI,
1653); the dresses themselves are termed 'cositas de capricho'
(XXXVIII, 1659) corresponding to the architectural 'caprichos'
of the servants' quarters or the 'caprichosas malquerencias'
(XXXI, 1643) Rosalía occasionally feels for her husband.

Thiers's postulation of the work ethic is echoed by Refugio
who considers herself an exception in the general Madrid sloth
and deceit: 'yo no engaño a nadie; yo vivo de mi trabajo. Pero
vosotras engañáis a medio mundo y queréis hacer vestidos de
seda con el pan del pobre' (XLVI, 1675). Refugio works undeniably hard at selling her fashions, but in the context of Madrid
society in 1868 and the limited economic and social usefulness
of the profession she has chosen, the wisdom of her actions is
open to grave doubts; these are fully confirmed by the ultimate
failure of the venture. A few individuals are shown to work

[25] Interestingly, at the same time in his *La Prensa* article on the
recent Fernán Núñez ball, Galdós had noted, tongue in cheek: 'Muchos
censuran estas fiestas por el dineral que se gasta en ellas inútilmente,
dinero que aplicado a objetos de mayor interés sería reproductivo...
Fuera de que es imposible y económicamente absurdo reglamentar el
empleo que cada cual quiera dar a su peculio, las artes e industrias
suntuarias, que dan circulación y vida a inmensos capitales, *no existirían
sin estas demandas constantes del capricho y de la frivolidad, elemento
fatal, imprescindible de toda sociedad*', Shoemaker, *Las cartas desconocidas*, pp. 70-1; my italics.

in the novel: Torquemada and Golfín display a good capitalist spirit, but their fruitful, individual labours in these social services do not create future wealth and prosperity for society as a whole.

The financial survival of the Bringas family in *Tormento* had been achieved in two ways: extreme domestic thrift and sponging on wealthy relations like Agustín, or the Queen, the system of 'recomendaciones'. In *La de Bringas* Rosalía's spending habits nullify the first course, whilst Agustín's move to Bordeaux and the Queen's absence for the summer close the second avenue. Refugio's emphatic remark to Rosalía is most pertinent: 'Si estuviera aquí la *Señora*, no pasaría usted esos apurillos, porque con echarse a sus pies y llorarle un poco ...' (XLVII, 1676). This refined parasitism is no better than street begging (Francisco, in fact, pleads poverty to Golfín, XXXII, 1646), and is put into sharper focus by Alfonsín's brazen requests for money to Pez and the Queen (XXVIII, 1638), the farcical Maundy Thursday meal for the two dozen street beggars, and Milagros's and Rosalía's absurd envy of beggars when faced with a seemingly insurmountable financial crisis (XXIV, 1630; XXIX, 1640).

Another form of parasitism is theft, which, according to Cándida, is rife in the Palace (XIX, 1619). In *Tormento* Francisco's new overcoat had been stolen at a Palace ball. Milagros half seriously considers theft as a remedy in a moment of despair: 'en un caso como éste me figuro que sería capaz hasta de apropiarme lo ajeno ..., se entiende, con propósito de devolver' (XXIV, 1630). Avoiding the payment of tax on imported goods like clothes is considered by Pez, Milagros and other Palace society members not as a crime but as a virtue, with the State now cast in the role of the robber and criminal: 'Está ya en nuestras costumbres y parece una quijotería el mirar por la Renta. Es genuinamente español esto de ver en el Estado, el ladrón legal, el ladrón permanente, el ladrón histórico' (XXXVI, 1654). The problem of obtaining money is of paramount importance to these Palace characters. The solution, however difficult to find, requires a complex series of practical manoeuvres and mental adjustments. Yet in the last resort the solution can be easily supplied if principles of moral behaviour are ignored, as the respective stories of Milagros, Refugio and Rosalía demonstrate.

c) *Sex*

Considering the prominence Galdós gave to the question of adultery in his 1870 manifesto (7, pp. 123-4), his delicate treatment of Rosalía's and Pez's relationship, whose final nature some critics have misinterpreted *(12)*, [26] would be surprising if the novel's basic pattern were not one of perplexing ambiguities. Indeed, the theme of adultery, contrary to Palley's view (*40*, p. 341), is not in itself important, despite its widespread occurrence within this Palace society. For Rosalía it is only a means to an end. More important still, she is not attracted by Pez's sexual prowess, rather by his external display of clothes, his pompous rhetorical language and his position as a high-ranking Civil Servant (XXIV-V, 1631). Rosalía really sublimates her sexual needs in her obsession for clothes (*38*, p. 52) as can be clearly seen on her first visit to Sobrino Hermanos: 'En su casa no pudo apartar de la imaginación todo aquel día y toda la noche la dichosa manteleta, y de tal modo arrebataba su sangre el ardor del deseo, que temió un ataquillo de erisipela si no lo saciaba.' Next day the two women return to the shop: 'La preferida [the shawl] apareció con su forma elegante y su lujosa pasamanería, en la cual las centellicas negras del abalorio, temblando entre felpas, confirmaban todo lo que los poetas han dicho del manto de la noche. Rosalía hubo de sentir frío en el pecho, ardor en las sienes, y en sus hombros los nervios le sugirieron tan al vivo la sensación del contacto y peso de la manteleta, que creyó llevarla ya puesta' (X, 1603). The physiological details of Rosalía's reactions, together with nocturnal references and the anthropomorphization of the garment, clearly point to a physical experience comparable to sexual orgasm. [27]

[26] See also Tréverret, 'Le Roman et le réalisme', p. 166.
[27] Werner Sombart, *Luxury and Capitalism* (Ann Arbor: University of Michigan, 1967), pp. 60-1, claimed that human sexuality lies at the root of the desire to possess luxury items.

d) *Religion*

This obsession with clothes also assumes religious proportions: 'La de Bringas, que en esta época de nuestra historia se había apasionado grandemente por los vestidos, elevó a Milagros en su alma un verdadero altar' (IX, 1601). The addition of the Garden of Eden image, grotesquely modernized ('Nada, nada ..., cuesta trabajo creer que aquello de doña Eva sea tan remoto. Digan lo que quieran, debió de pasar ayer, según está de fresquito y palpitante el tal suceso. Parece que lo han traído los periódicos de anoche', IX, 1601) deflates and ridicules this exaggerated veneration for clothes. Clothes and sex have become the respective religions of these two characters. The Christian religion appears only in a hollow external form: the farcical Maundy Thursday ceremony, Milagros's sponsored devotions (XVIII, 1617) are all occasions to exhibit the latest fashions. [28] Nor are the external appearances of religious buildings a sure indicator of virtuous practices within: the Chapel cupola, significantly one of over fifty religious buildings visible on the Madrid sky-line (IV, 1593), dominates the Palace but only serves to conceal disordered structures and immoral behaviour; religious publishing houses also give Refugio's den of prostitution an air of respectability (XLV, 1671). The day of her adultery with Pez, Rosalía pretends to Francisco that she is going to Mass, 'como lo demostraba el devocionario con tapas de nácar que llevara en la mano' (XLIII, 1669). Isabelita's collection of religious figures reflects 'el arte parisiense [que] representa las cosas santas con el mismo estilo de los figurines de modas' (XL, 1663). Carolina Pez's apparent devotion, distorted by her husband's resentment, also has very little to do

---

[28] Galdós commits a chronological inaccuracy when he places the Maundy Thursday 'Comida de los Pobres' in the Salón de Columnas. This room had been used for such a purpose only after the death of Alfonso XII's first wife, María de las Mercedes, in 1878; see Mrs Steuart Erskine, *Madrid: Past and Present* (London: the Bodley Head, 1922), pp. 30-1. Galdós's description of the ceremony corresponds to the events of 1884; see Mercedes Agulló y Cobo, *Madrid en sus diarios, IV (1876-1890)* (Madrid: Instituto de Estudios Madrileños, 1971), pp. 333-4.

with the spirit as opposed to the external forms of religion. She errs in the opposite direction. Pez cynically sums up his pragmatic reasons for this discrepancy between appearances and reality: 'Siempre había defendido la Religión, y le parecía muy bien que los gobiernos la protegieran, persiguiendo a los difamadores de ella. Llegaba hasta admitir, como indispensable en el régimen político de su tiempo, la mojigatería del Estado, pero la mojigatería privada le reventaba' (XIII, 1608).

Fashions, money, sex and religion are the major preoccupations of this Palace society in descending order of importance. In fact, one might join them together in a vicious circle of interests. Religion and fashion, at opposite extremes, meet full circle when religion furnishes an important opportunity for these characters to indulge their true religion of clothes. For this to take place, money is needed and that may be readily available only through the sale of one's body. Thus, these social photographic records are arranged in a meaningful and causal relationship that provides a framework for Galdós to develop his story and at the same time to illustrate his major theme of the distorted relationship between outer appearances and true underlying reality. Moreover, this whirl of obsessions also involved its leaders, Isabel and her husband Francisco de Asís, and Galdós could not avoid their inclusion in the novel if he were not to falsify the historical value of his social pictures.

7. 'La de Bringas' as an 'episodio nacional'

G ALDÓS's presentation of the historical material is surrounded by the same degree of ambiguity that accompanies
other features of the novel. *La de Bringas* relates the story of
people who live and work in the Palace; it is set for the most
part within the Palace precincts; the public events that lead
to the Revolution of September play an important part in the
development of the fiction, constituting one of the four principal
threads of action (see Chapter 5). Furthermore, the story of
Rosalía's moral downfall because of reckless spending has been
rightly considered by critics *(14, 46)* as a reflection of the story
of Queen Isabel's life. Yet despite these important indicators
of a second layer of reference in the novel, a second story being
narrated, the Monarchs never make a full, direct appearance
as the reader expects. [29] Their sole appearance — at the Maundy
Thursday ceremony in the Salón de Columnas — is exceedingly
distanced, both in its physical location and its verbal description. This reticence, albeit not complete enough for the Con-
servative Alfonso *(24)*, might well have been due to a tactful,
newly-discovered respect by Galdós for the restored Bourbons:
in an 1868 newspaper article he had been brutally sarcastic
towards members of the recently deposed dynasty. [30]

The real key to the understanding of this enigmatic presentation, however, lies in Galdós's concept of the rôle of political
history in his new type of social novel inaugurated in the 'serie
contemporánea'. From *La desheredada* to *Miau* Galdós manages through his fictional story to suggest the major outline of

[29] Federico Sopeña Ibáñez, *Arte y sociedad en Galdós* (Madrid:
Gredos, 1970), p. 71.
[30] Shoemaker, *Los artículos de Galdós en 'La Nación'*, pp. 541-4.

the historical period in question. This technique, that I hesitate
to label as historical allegory, consists of a number of features:
dropping occasional allusions to the historical events; creating
parallels between certain fictional and historical episodes and
characters; and, finally, employing at important junctures a
single word or phrase that can also suggest, by a kind of short-
hand, a whole political situation without further elaboration.
The common denominator of all these devices is indirectness:
the second level of historical story is never presented directly
to the reader; it is always distanced.

Despite this brevity of style, coverage of political developments in *La de Bringas* is extremely comprehensive and accurate (*16,* p. 123): rumours of a revolution increase throughout 1868 (III, 1591; XXXIV, 1651; XLIII, 1668; XLVII,
1676); the Democrats' ultimatum to the Government of González Bravo in July (XXXVI, 1654) is followed by the exile of
the Generals in the same month and the move of the Court
to La Granja and then to Lequeitio. Prim's sojourn in Vichy,
González Bravo's illness and the visit of the Carlist leader
Cabrera to Don Carlos in London are minor details also
included (XXVII, 1637). In Chapters XLVIII to L, a profusion
of details records the advance of the revolutionaries from Cádiz to their ultimate objective of Madrid and the subsequent
establishment of the Provisional Government in October of
1868.

Throughout Galdós maintains an elongated perspective:
developments are related through the conversations or news-
paper-readings of the fictional characters and this distancing is
often increased by the actual physical location from which
these scenes are presented, as, for example, when Cándida
reports the arrest of the Generals to Francisco immediately
before his loss of sight: the whole scene is presented from the
position of Rosalía who is half listening to the conversation
from another room. Other means of distorting the historical
account include the juxtaposition of other more trivial conversation subjects: 'como brillaban las lentejuelas de algunos
abanicos, así relucían los conceptos uno tras otro ...: El verano
se anticipaba aquel año y sería muy cruel ... Los generales

habían llegado a Canarias ... Prim estaba en Vichy ... la
Reina iría a La Granja y después a Lequeitio ... Se em-
pezaban a llevar las colas algo recogidas, y para baños, las
colas estaban ya proscritas ... González Bravo estaba malo del
estómago ... Cabrera había ido a ver al *Niño Terso*' (XXVII,
1637).

Pez's sexual frustration (XXXVI, 1653-4) or concern for
Francisco's mental well-being (XXIV, 1631), the timidity of the
eyewitness Paquito (XLIX, 1680), significantly colour and dis-
tort other relations of historical events. This consistently un-
natural perspective is even maintained during the revolutionaries' take-over of the Royal Palace. Though a direct description
is possible and expected by the reader, Galdós prefers to filter
developments through the absurdly comical reports of Cándida
and Paquito, and Francisco's paranoiac reactions: 'No crea
usted, señor don Francisco, unos pobrecillos, almas de Dios ...
Como no nos manden acá otros descamisados que ésos, ya po-
demos echarnos a dormir. Algunos se subieron a las habita-
ciones Reales, y andaban por allí hechos unos bobos, mirando
a los techos ... En fin, es una risa. Baje usted y verá, verá ...
¿Matar? Sí, acaso alguna paloma. Dos o tres de ellos se han
entretenido en cazar a nuestras inocentes vecinas; pero con
muy mala fortuna. Los revolucionarios tienen mala puntería'
(XLIX, 1681). The distorted narrative perspective is thus highly
appropriate to convey the exaggerated, inauthentic approach to
reality of Francisco and the other characters. Furthermore, it
suits the nature of the event itself: the Revolution of 1868 was
a most peaceful change of regimes *(1; 3)*, as the final chapter
of *La de Bringas* convincingly demonstrates: Pez and the great
majority of the Palace servants are kept on by the Provisional
Government with only a few obstinate monarchists like Francisco abandoning their positions. Thus the development of the
political material fits into the novel's overall pattern of baffling
perspectives. Having constantly threatened to throw the country
into civil war, the Revolution finally achieves absurdly little:
the resignation of a few officials. Like the Palace structures
and developments in the story of the Bringas family, Spanish
politics is governed by whim, chance (XII, 1606), that produces
no change of substance. Hence the narrator's caustic comment

on Rosalía's vision of a new order to be brought in by the Revolution: 'Vendrían seguramente tiempos distintos, otra manera de ser, otras costumbres, la riqueza se iría de una parte a otra; habría grandes trastornos, caídas y elevaciones repentinas, sorpresas [an operative word in the Palace structure], prodigios y ese movimiento desordenado e irreflexivo de toda sociedad que ha vivido mucho tiempo impaciente de una transformación. Por lo que la Bringas dijo, fuera en estos términos o en otros que no recuerdo, vine a comprender que la imaginación de la insigne señora se dejaba ilusionar por lo desconocido' (L, 1682). Of Galdós's three novels directly related to the 1868 Revolution (*La Fontana de Oro* (1870), *La de los tristes destinos* (1907) are the other two) *La de Bringas* appears to be, by far, the least impassioned, lacking in explicit condemnation not only of the Bourbons but also of the failed Revolution. Yet this is only a trick of perspectivism. Through his indirect technique of narrating the Queen's story Galdós is able to make an effective criticism of the political events that took place.

In the same way the illusion of Isabel's absence from the novel fades when one notices the surprising number of occasions when her name is reported in the conversation of the fictional characters. However, the context of these references is most significant: by and large they occur, not in the reports of Court activities, but as part of the schemes hatched by these characters to secure more perquisites and privileges from their royal mistress. Francisco will rely on her for material for his planned wardrobe (XXV, 1633), for free train tickets to go on holiday (XXVI, 1634), for double pay in July (XXVI, 1634), or recouped pay (XLII, 1667) and, had the Queen been in Madrid, also for the payment of Golfín's bill (XXXVII, 1657). Similarly, Rosalía would have asked the Queen for a summer apartment in La Granja (XXXVII, 1655) and, like Milagros (XIX, 1620) would have thrown herself at the Sovereign's feet, had she been in Madrid, to ask for financial help (XLVII, 1676).

The Queen's involvement in the main matter of the novel is made even more evident when Rosalía uses her mistress's well-known munificence (2, pp. 176-8) as an excuse to explain

her purchase of the shawl, an excuse that she has used countless
times before:

> Aquí de las casualidades. Hallándose Rosalía en la Cá-
> mara Real en el momento que destapaban unas cajas
> recién llegadas de París, la Reina se probó un canesú
> que le venía estrecho, un cuerpo que le estaba ancho ...
> Luego, de una caja preciosa forrada de cretona por dentro
> y por fuera ..., una tela que parecía rasete ..., sacaron
> tres manteletas. Una de ellas le caía maravillosamente a
> Su Majestad; las otras dos, no. 'Ponte ésa, Rosaliita ...
> ¿Qué tal? Ni pintada.' En efecto, ni con medida estu-
> viera mejor. '¡Qué bien, qué bien! ... A ver, vuélvete ...
> ¿Sabes que me da no sé qué de quitártela? No, no te la
> quites ...' 'Pero, señora, por amor de Dios ...' 'No, dé-
> jala. Es tuya por derecho de conquista. ¡Es que tienes
> un cuerpo ...! Úsala en mi nombre, y no se hable más
> de ello.' De esta manera tan gallarda obsequiaba a sus
> amigas la graciosa Soberana ... Faltó poco para que a
> mi buen Thiers se le saltaran las lágrimas oyendo el bien
> contado relato. (XI, 1604) [31]

The familiar language put into the Queen's mouth by Rosalía
also reduces the Monarch to the level of the fictional characters.
Indeed, the roles seem dangerously reversed most of the time:
mistress becomes servant and vice-versa *(28)* as Refugio's references to the Queen in her ultimate conversation with Rosalía
show (XLVII, 1676). The Queen's involvement in the world of
her subjects becomes more serious, although still presented
indirectly from a distance, when she is reported by the narrator to have paid off Cándida's debts and to have given her
an apartment in the Palace (VI, 1595), to have written recommendations and excuses for Tula's worthless offspring (VII,
1596), and to have delighted in the malapropisms of her loyal
General Minio (VI, 1596). Her faulty judgement, her misuse
of time that could have been better devoted to State affairs, are
thus additional defects that emerge in Galdós's picture. She is

[31] Pedro de Répide, *Isabel II, reina de España,* 2nd ed. (Madrid:
Espasa-Calpe, 1932), pp. 152-5, cites a similar, historical episode.

no worse than her subjects around her, Galdós suggests, but
then she is no better either, when she should have been, and
that is serious criticism indeed. Unfortunately, this is our only
perspective — a disparaging one — on the Queen. None the less,
her picture has still not yet taken on the dimensions of Valle-
Inclán's caricature in the *Ruedo ibérico*. [32]

Having integrated his political material into the structure
and style of the novel, Galdós now gives it additional thematic
significance by twinning certain historical events with important
developments in the fiction. Francisco's sudden loss of sight
occurs just as Cándida is reporting the news of the Generals'
banishment to the Canary Islands. The obvious implication is
that Francisco's blindness is comparable to the political short-
sightedness shown by the González Bravo Government in this
action and also that the event will have tragic repercussions for
Francisco (as it does), just as the 7 July edict led to the downfall of González Bravo's government. [33] Rosalía's relationship
with Pez blossoms on their Spring walks with the children in
the Retiro; as they leave the park, the narrator observes: 'Ya
estaban descuajadas las famosas alamedas de castaños de In-
dias, quitada la verja y puestos a la venta los terrenos, opera-
ción que se llamó *rasgo*. Esta palabra fue funesta para la Mo-
narquía, árbol a quien no le valió ser más antiguo que los
castaños, porque también me lo descuajaron e hicieron leña de
él' (XVII, 1614). Just as Isabel's absurd generosity to the Spanish nation in 1865 became in the subsequent political backlash
led by Castelar an important stage in her eventual downfall,
so this apparently innocent stroll with Pez will also have disas-
trous consequences for Rosalía. Her final determination to become a high-class prostitute ('Esquivando el trato de Peces,

---

[32] See Alison Sinclair, *Valle-Inclán's 'Ruedo Ibérico': a Popular
View of Revolution* (London: Tamesis, 1977), pp. 27-87. For Galdós's
necrology on Queen Isabel, see 'La reina Isabel', VI, 1426-32.

[33] Francisco's attitude is symptomatic: Government officials blindly
believed in the loyalty of the Armed Forces and the impossibility of
revolution right up to 18 September; see Fernando Díaz-Plaja, *La historia de España en sus documentos: el siglo XIX* (Madrid: Instituto de
Estudios Políticos, 1954), pp. 335-6.

Tellerías y gente de poco más o menos, buscaría más sólidos y eficaces apoyos en los Fúcares, los Trujillos, los Cimarras y otras familias de la aristocracia positiva', XLVIII, 1680) is immediately followed by more serious news about the advance of the revolutionaries: 'era el acabamiento del mundo ... Don Francisco oyó, gimiendo, que también se pronunciaban Béjar, Santoña, Santander y otras plazas' (XLIX, 1680). The inference is that Rosalía's moral fall parallels the final political (and earlier moral) fall of Queen Isabel (*14*, pp. 120-5). This outcome had already been anticipated by the initial description of Rosalía's obsession for clothes: 'hace en el mundo más estragos que las revoluciones' (X, 1602).

The final device Galdós uses to integrate the political material into the rest of the novel is to employ politically or historically suggestive words from time to time. His use of expressions like 'destierro' (XXXVII, 1655; XL, 1662), 'desterrado' (XIII, 1608), 'proscrita' (XXXVIII, 1659), 'emancipación' (XXXIII, 1648), 'emanciparse' (XLI, 1664), all in non-political contexts, takes on an extra meaning when considered alongside the political banishments and imprisonments of the same days. The personal 'libertad' Rosalía longs for so much (XXIX, 1640) is echoed on the political level by Refugio: 'habrá libertad, libertades' (XLVII, 1676). Galdós is almost explicit on one occasion: 'los madrileños que pasan el verano en la Villa son verdaderos desterrados, los proscritos, y su único consuelo es decir que beben la mejor agua del mundo' (XXXVIII, 1658).

Imagery can also join the two worlds of fiction and history: Rosalía's virtue is likened to a vulnerable fortress (XLI, 1665) comparable to that of the Royal Palace at the end (L, 1683). Another image is given its historical counterpoint: the Palace is likened to a ship tossed about by the waves (IV, 1593); its occupants see their political safety in the expulsion of the rebellious generals by ship to the Canary Islands. However, their final downfall is determined by the revolt of the Navy and the ferrying of Prim and the other conspirators to Cádiz: '¡Qué infamia! ¡La Marina española! ... Pero ¿cómo? Ya se ve; en cuanto ha tenido buques' (XLVIII, 1679) is their desperate comment once the Revolution breaks out. In an inversion of the technique, the precipice on which Pez sees the country poised (XXVII, 1637) recalls the view of the outside world from the Palace's third floor: 'el plano superior del cornisamento de Palacio [parecía] un ancho puente sobre el precipicio, por donde podría correr con holgura quien no padeciera vértigos' (IV, 1593). Despite the number of these devices, the historical outlines of the period can still be relegated as mere background decoration. To fully weld it to his fiction and ensure that it also receives the same distorting treatment as other elements in the novel, Galdós had to make the principal invented characters reflect some of the features of the historical personages.

8. *Characterization*

a) *Rosalía*

HER pretty, plumpish figure (XIII, 1607; XXIII, 1628) along
with the occasional dilation of her nostrils (XXV, 1632;
XXXIX, 1660) or her Palace-like dimensions in Isabelita's second dream (XXXIV, 1651) are exaggerated physical features
that allow Rosalía to be viewed as an image of the Queen and
her story to be interpreted as a parable or allegory of the life
of Isabel. That is certainly one purpose of the physical twinning; another is surely to ridicule the absurd pretensions of
this Palace servant. Herein lies the relevance of other references
to famous historical or literary female figures: the Empress
Josephine (XVII, 1615), Eve (IX, 1601), and in *Tormento* to a
goddess in a Rubens picture: 'se había comparado tantas veces
con los tipos de Rubens, que por un fenómeno de costumbre
y de asimilación, siempre que se nombraba al insigne flamenco,
creía que mentaban a alguno de la familia ... Entiéndase bien,
de la familia de Pipaón de la Barca' (II, 1476). This surname is
a source of genealogical fantasy-building; the reality is more
prosaic: 'Observaciones precisas nos dan a conocer que Rosalía no carecía de títulos para afiliarse, por la línea materna,
en esa nobleza pobre y servil que ha brillado en los cargos
palatinos de poca importancia' (II, 1475). Rosalía is a daughter
of the Palace who returns home in *La de Bringas,* but not as
the noble figure of religious, artistic or historical fantasy that
she and the narrator imagine at times. These comparisons are
thus comic, ironic.

Montesinos (*16,* p. 131) and Gullón (*14*) believe that Rosalía's obsession with clothes in *La de Bringas* is due to the Palace surroundings and the political situation. Yet this determi-
nistic view of Rosalía's character is too restrictive. The evidence
provided by *Tormento* helps to gain a more balanced pers-

pective. As Ricard has noted (*32*, pp. 50-1), there are a number of surprising differences between the Rosalías of the two novels. On the other had, the progression from dutiful housewife is one to spendthrift adulteress in the other is not so sudden or unprepared. In *Tormento,* once she is aware of Amparo's past affair with Pedro Polo, believing Agustín will forget Amparo, she seriously tries to seduce Agustín for her own advantage, with a careful display of clothes and neat appearance:

> Al decir esto y lo que siguió, cualquiera que atentamente observara a Rosalía podría haber sorprendido en ella, junto con el deseo de convencer a su primo, el no menos vivo de hacer patente su hermosura, realzada en aquella ocasión por el esmero del vestir y por los aliños y adornos de buscada oportunidad. Cómo enseñaba sus blancos dientes, cómo contorneaba su cuello, cómo se erguía para dar a su bien fajada cintura esbeltez momentánea, eran detalles que tú y yo, lector amigo, habríamos reparado, mas no Caballero, por la situación en que su espíritu se hallaba. (XXXV, 1572)

This passage offers us an anticipatory glimpse of the fateful combination of two urges (ostentation and material ambition) that will destroy Rosalía in the second novel. Towards the end of the latter, the narrator discloses that ten years previously Rosalía, although married, had been wooed unsuccessfully by philandering aristocrats like the Marqués de Fúcar (XLI, 1664). The point Galdós is trying to establish is that Rosalía has flirted before with the possiblity of adultery to improve her social position. Her fall at the end of *La de Bringas* is not the result of her taking up residence in the Palace (although the atmosphere there clearly is no disincentive to such an action) but rather of her inner character, as he stresses on a couple of occasions (IX, 1601 ; XXXVI, 1653).

It is all too easy to represent Rosalía as some kind of ogre (*16*, p. 276). Yet she is particularly attentive to her children at all times (*38*), and during her husband's relapse is genuinely upset and tends him with loving care (XXXI, 1644). She can also be disconcertingly perceptive about the social pretensions of her friends and even of herself; the narrator calls our attention to the surprising wisdom of her commentaries on the Tellería household (XIV, 1610), Pez's lifestyle (XXXI, 1643), and her own inferiority to Francisco (XLIV, 1670). These redeeming features made her for Alas (*23*, p. 130) Galdós's most successful female character to date. However, Galdós does not seem concerned to create a fully rounded human character so much as to emphasize the troubling mixture of opposing qualities in her character and the sudden shifts of balance between those qualities that occur at times: 'Viendo a su esposo tan decaído y maltrecho, se reverdeció en Rosalía el cariño de otros tiempos; y el aprecio en que siempre le tenía depurábase de caprichosas malquerencias *para resurgir grande y cordial,* tocando en veneración' (my italics; XXXI, 1643). These swift sudden changes in character, the result of conflicting pressures, often cause Rosalía to appear to be in a highly emotional state, whether it be one of anxiety over Francisco's possible discovery of her secret (XI, 1604; XVIII, 1616), or one of embarrassment at Pez's advances and their final adultery (XXXV, 1653; XLII, 1669) and at her deeply humiliating visit to Refugio (XLVIII, 1678). In these states of physical and emotional tension she often appeals to the Deity (XVI, 1614; XIX, 1621; XX, 1622; XXI, 1623; XLI, 1664) and sometimes in an absurdly exaggerated fashion: 'Rosalía invocó a todos los santos, a todas las Vírgenes, a la Santísima Trinidad, y aun se cree que hizo alguna promesa a Santa Rita si la sacaba en bien de aquel apuro ... Aunque [Francisco] solía repasar los billetes sólo por gusto, en aquella ocasión no lo hizo sabe Dios por qué. Quizás todas aquellas invocaciones que la señora hizo a los santos obtuvieron buena acogida, y algún ángel inspiró al ratoncito Pérez la idea de dejar para otra vez el recuento de sus ahorros' (XXXIII, 1648-9). The irony of these desperate invocations from an irreligious person is further increased by Milagros's and Francisco's exalted references to her as an angel (XXXIII, 1645; XXXI, 1644).

Thus, for most of the novel, Rosalía's physical features, their likeness to those of other famous females, her emotional states and language are pencilled in with exaggerated, disproportionate contours, intersected by the occasional perplexing relapses into perceptive honesty and kind affection. However, at the end Rosalía appears a changed woman, no longer subject to the shifts of moods or emotional instability. The final view of her is important: 'Serena y un tanto majestuosa, Rosalía no dijo una palabra en todo el trayecto desde la casa a la Plaza de Oriente, mas de sus ojos elocuentes se desprendía una convicción orgullosa, la conciencia de su papel de piedra angular de la casa en tan aflictivas circunstancias' (L, 1683). The tension and anxiety have disappeared from the surface; Rosalía is calm, at peace with herself, because her occasional moral sense, her humanity, has finally disappeared. The person has finally become a hollow mask: the gap between pretence and probity has irremediably widened: 'Si en la estimación que por él sentía [por Francisco] había una baja considerable, las formas externas del respeto acusaban cierto refinamiento y estudio' (XLVIII, 1678). The actress has finally forgotten her real identity and learnt the part dictated by her guiding 'amor propio', the basic character defect that Galdós had identified upon her first appearance in *Tormento*: 'su flaco era cierta manía nobiliaria' (II, 1475). When Milagros's stunning attack on her 'cursilería' should have caused her to re-examine her conduct (XLVIII, 1678), her wounded 'amor propio', far from disappearing, only increases in strength, to the reader's surprise. At the end of the novel Rosalía is a balloon of hollow social pretence with no redeeming affection: the moral change now justifies the exaggerated physical contours. However, behind this balloon of vanity, propelling it along its confirmed path, is the final secret of Rosalía's character: her fertile imagination (XV, 1611), examples of which we noted in Chapter 2. Her reliance on this dangerous faculty becomes evident at the end of the novel, when she looks forward to the Revolution with unrealistic expectations: 'La revolución era cosa mala, según decían todos; pero también era lo desconocido, y lo desconocido atrae las imaginaciones exaltadas, y seduce a los que se han creado en su vida una situación irregular. Vendrían otros tiempos; otro modo de ser, algo nuevo, estupendo y que diera juego. "En fin —pensaba ella— veremos eso"' (XLVIII, 1679). (Her 'mente soñadora' also promises her prosperous future liaisons.) That dangerously defective inner vision, the imagination, thus finally obliterates those partial visions of reality that at odd times had made Rosalía more worthy of consideration as a human being.

b) *Francisco*

Though he did not follow Castro y Serrano's advice (*16*, p. 276; see also *28*) and call his novel *Los Bringas*, Galdós made Francisco equal in prominence and treatment to Rosalía. For instance, he too is compared to a number of famous (male) figures. However, the latter are drawn, not from the fantasy world of myth, art or literature (as in the case of most of Rosalía's comparisons) but from the real world of national and international political history. The first analogy is suggested by Francisco's surname: his historical namesake had been an important Liberal conspirator during the last decade of Fernando VII's reign (*39*). Although Galdós denies this comparison in *Tormento* (II, 1474-5), there is every reason to believe that he intended it. Secondly, Francisco's physical appearance recalls that of the French statesman, Adolphe Thiers (II, 1477). Thirdly, a minor comparison to Napoleon in *Tormento* (III, 1478) is continued in *La de Bringas* when Rosalía indirectly compares herself to the Empress Josephine (XVII, 1615). [34] Finally, Francisco's Christian name also calls to mind that of the Royal Consort, Francisco de Asís. Both are ultra-right-wingers in political ideology and are associated in Isabelita's initial nightmare: 'Pero mucho más bonito estaría su papá cuando se hiciese caballero del Santo Sepulcro. El Rey tenía empeño en ello, y le había prometido regalarle el uniforme con todos los accesorios de espada, espuelas y demás' (VIII, 1600). Francisco is also smaller and considerably older than Rosalía (by 15 years). Francisco de Asís, by comparison, was only eight years older than his wife; physically, he was slimmer and shorter too. Sexual

---

[34] During the Paris Commune of 1870 Thiers was often likened to Napoleon; see Pierre Descaves, *Monsieur Thiers* (Paris: La Table Ronde, 1960), p. 108. The Napoleonic comparisons are not inappropriate in the context of the Madrid Royal Palace where the Emperor had visited his brother, Joseph, in 1809, as Galdós had already chronicled in *Napoleón, en Chamartín* (1874).

dissatisfaction may well be one of the unconscious reasons for Rosalía's growing boredom with Francisco; certainly her reminiscences of the honeymoon spent in unpoetic Navalcarnero with the suggestive Freudian reference to Francisco's lack of skill with the hunting rifle (XXIX, 1640) are significant in this regard. Naturally, Galdós has not made the physical parallel rigidly exact in every detail; for example, he does not suggest that Francisco Bringas had any homosexual tendencies as Paco de Asís clearly did. None the less, there are enough indicators to suggest that Galdós did create the physical outline of his principal couple with the Queen and her consort in mind. Fiction and history are further joined by the common denominator of Marfori: Isabel's current lover is Francisco's superior, the Intendente, mentioned only by title, never by name in the novel. Surely the purpose behind all of these historical parallels is to ridicule the importance of Bringas: in name and appearance he resembles some great figures of world history. In reality, however, there can be no comparison, for Bringas lacks the inner qualities of the renowned counterparts. Bringas is only an insignificant Palace servant who spends all his time on the absurdly futile hair-picture.

Yet, like Rosalía, Francisco can show on occasions some human feelings and qualities which diminish his stature as a caricature and evoke the more normal image presented in *Tormento*. He is willing to let Rosalía buy some new clothes (XXXI, 1645) and thinks of her well-being in the overheated rooms in the summer (XXV, 1632). These moments of tender consideration are the product of his illness and are short-lived, fading as quickly as his vision returns. But this 'niño senil' (XXXIII, 1647) also suffers, like his wife, from excessive emotionalism, which, though understandable during his illness, constitutes a regular and disquieting feature of his personality at other times. After conceiving the idea of making the hair-picture for the Pez family, he leaves their house 'febril y temblequeante. Tenía la enfermedad epiléptica de la gestión artística. La obra, recién encarnada en su mente, anunciaba ya con íntimos rebullicios que era un ser vivo, y se desarrollaba potentísima oprimiendo las paredes del cerebro y excitando los pares nerviosos, que llevaban inexplicables sensaciones de ahogo

a la respiración, a la epidermis hormiguilla, a las extremidades
desasosiego, y al ser todo impaciencia, temores, no sé qué
más . . . ' (II, 1589). He shudders with fear at the thought of the
Revolution (III, 1591), goes delirious with delight when told
that the Generals have been exiled to the Canaries (XXX, 1642),
and finally relapses into a permanent state of shock and paranoiac fear when the militia takes over the Palace. Our final
picture of Francisco is of a very sick man: 'apoyado en el
brazo de su señora, andaba con lentitud, la vista perturbada,
indecisa el habla' (L, 1683). Questions of money always upset
him because he hates spending. The costs of his treatment from
Golfín are cause for extreme agitation: he confesses that he
suffered an epileptic fit worrying about the final figure
(XXXVII, 1656). At 8,000 reales it is two hundred and forty
times more than the original cost of the hair-picture: 'la realidad había partido la diferencia entre estas dos sumas ilusorias'
(the 4,000 and 16,000 reales that he had alternately imagined;
XXXVII, 1657). In *Tormento* he had also been presented as
a thrifty person. This quality has become distorted in the second
novel because he now values his social and economic position
even more highly: 'Tal canonjía [the promotion to the Palace]
realizaba las aspiraciones de toda su vida, y no *cambiara Thiers
aquel su puesto tan alto, seguro y respetuoso, por la silla del
Primado de las Españas*' (my italics; V, 1591). Economizing
has now become a mania for Francisco, as clothes have become
a passion for Rosalía. Their respective distortions are fuelled
and maintained by paranoiac fear of anything that threatens
the obsession. Physical and emotional stress are the inevitable
consequences.

c) *Milagros*

Though Castro y Serrano (*16*, p. 276) erred in viewing Milagros as the central character of the novel, her importance is
not to be minimized. Her responsibility for encouraging Rosalía
to indulge her passion for clothes-buying with its ultimate consequences is considerable indeed. Rosalía's story would not have
been possible without the decisive influence of her friend at
this juncture in her life. At the same time Galdós also intends

that the reader should consider Milagros as a reflection or
mirror of Rosalía's character. More importantly, within the
fiction she is also meant to offer a lesson for Rosalía herself:
Rosalía does on one occasion perceive the true nature of Milagros's character (XIV, 1610) but fails to apply the lesson to
her own position. Like Rosalía, Milagros is prone to extremes
of emotion, generally feigned for the purpose of eliciting funds
from her friend, and for which the only solution seems to lie in
divine intervention (hence the irony of her name; XIX, 1619-20;
XXIII, 1629; XXX, 1641-2). Physically too, with her cleverly
applied make-up whose description recalls the appearance of
the Palace structure (IX, 1601), she seems to anticipate Rosalía's future decline.

d) *Cándida*

At an even more advanced stage of decay, as Galdós's careful manipulation of references to other novels brings out perfectly clearly, is Cándida who appears to help people at critical
moments of need: the narrator and Pez, when lost in the Palace
labyrinth; Rosalía, when she wants to pawn the candelabra;
and the Bringas family, when they are overcome by the shock
of Francisco's illness, or when they barricade themselves in the
apartment after the militia's take-over of the Palace. This duty
in the development of the story draws attention to her possible
importance for the novel's theme: in fact, like Milagros, she is
a mirror figure for Rosalía and the reader. The narrator's naive
assumption that Cándida is one of the Queen's confidantes may
be excusable (V, 1594); Rosalía, on the other hand, deliberately
chooses to ignore the reality of Cándida's current position,
failing to apply its relevance for her own situation: 'Rosalía
sentía hacia ella [Cándida] respetuoso afecto y la oía siempre
con sumisión, conceptuándola como gran autoridad en materias
sociales y en toda suerte de elegancias. A los ojos de la señora
de Thiers, el brillantísimo pasado de Cándida había dejado, al
borrarse del tiempo, resplandores de prestigio y nobleza en
torno al busto romano y al tieso empaque de la ilustre viuda.
Esta aureola fascinaba a Rosalía, quien, extremando su respeto

a las majestades caídas, aparentaba tomar en serio aquello de
mi administrador, mis casas . . .' (VI, 1595).

e) *Refugio*

The final female figure in this series or Chinese box of reflecting characters, Refugio, shows, perhaps, the closest physical
resemblance to Rosalía and the Queen: she is short and buxom,
and also on occasions appears in a state of semi-undress (XLV,
1672) as was the Queen's wont (*2*, p. 175) and at times Rosalía's
(XIV, 1609). Refugio is also a distant cousin of Rosalía's, their
common ancestor having been a Palace servant (IV, 1480). In
Refugio's final confrontation with Rosalía, the allusions to
the Queen's absence from Madrid, and the references to Milagros's assessment of Rosalía's 'cursilería', also underline the
basic similarity in physique and moral attitude of these female
characters, a similarity that is reflected in the common designation (except for Cándida): 'La de Bringas', 'la Señora' (in the
companion 'episodio' the Queen is given the title 'la de los
tristes destinos'), 'la de Sánchez' (XLV, 1672) and 'la de Tellería' (XLVIII, 1678). The equalization of these characters is
clearly illustrated as well by Celestina's ambiguous relationship
to Refugio, and Rosalía's temporary duty as hairdresser and
wardrobe mistress to Refugio in this scene (*45*).

In keeping with the surprising perspectives of the novel,
Refugio, who has accurately summed up the faults of others in
Madrid, fails to apply the same insight to her own situation;
she is as guilty as the others of hiding her true life-style beneath
respectable appearances. We have already seen how her apartment is flanked by religious businesses. More enigmatically, she
had earlier told Rosalía: 'Vivo con unas señoras muy decentes,
que me quieren mucho. Hago una vida retirada' (XXVI, 1635).
Galdós also adroitly hints during her snatches of moral sermo-
nizing to Rosalía that these right-sounding observations are not
really the fruit of her own applied moral scrutiny, but rather
the memorized phrases of her friend, 'un caballero que yo conozco'. Refugio repeats her source so much (four times in one
and a half pages in the Aguilar edition) that Rosalía wonders
to herself: 'Pero ¿cuántos caballeros conoces tú, grandísimo

apunte?' (XLVII, 1676). The almost theatrical format of her recitation is also suggested by the narrator's remark: 'Al soltar esta retahíla con un énfasis y un calor que declaraban hallarse muy poseída de su asunto . . . ' (XLVI, 1675). Moreover, if Refugio were as truly concerned about Rosalía's future behaviour as she claims ('y le voy a dar un consejo . . . un buen consejo, para que vea que me intereso por la familia', XLVIII, 1677), why does she give Rosalía the money when she knows full well her cousin's behaviour and character? It is hard not to see personal spite and vindictiveness in her actions throughout this scene. In short, Refugio is as short-sighted about her own moral faults as the Queen, Rosalia, Milagros and others whom she is so ready to criticize and condemn.

Galdós's reiteration of traits in these female characters should not be construed as a sign of defective characterization: the women are sufficiently distinguished by individual mannerisms, temperament and intelligence. None the less, in his desire to point out the common moral attitudes of this group, Galdós does come very close to creating a common type. In Don Manuel Pez, this type is fully realized.

f) *Pez*

Continuing the characterization he had first made in *La desheredada*, Galdós exploits the comic possibilities of Pez's name and physical figure in *La de Bringas* with allusions to his need for a daily glass of water and frequent trips to distant spas. The most sustained example of this animalization occurs in the early description of Pez's submarine voyage through the Palace quarters. A repeated religious comparison to St Joseph increases the comic appeal of the figure, especially when he walks with Rosalía on the terrace of the Palace: 'La ninfa de Rubens, carnosa y redonda, y el espiritual San José, de levita y sin vara de azucenas, se sublimaban sobre aquel fondo arquitectónico' (XIII, 1607).

At the same time Pez is explicitly represented as a symbol of the Spanish Civil Service, the corrupt political system, and, above all, of the nation's spiritual attitude:

Aquellos ojos decían a todo el que los miraba: 'Soy la
expresión de esa España dormida, beatífica, que se goza
en ser juguete de los sucesos y en nada se mete con tal
que la dejen comer tranquila; que no anda, que nada
espera y vive de la ilusión del presente, mirando al cielo,
con una vara florecida en la mano; que se somete a todo
el que la quiere mandar, venga de donde viniere, y pro-
fesa el socialismo manso; que no entiende de ideas, ni
de acción, ni de nada que no sea soñar y digerir.' (XII,
1607)

Thus Pez stands as the representative of all the other characters in the novel who cover up their inner emptiness with a
dazzlingly impressive exterior, be it sartorial or verbal. Pez's
artificially immaculate appearance, which plays such a great
part in the seduction of Rosalía, serves also to establish the
final component of Galdós's extended, Chinese-box-like method
of characterization: 'Vestía este caballero casi casi como un
figurín. Daba gozo ver su extraordinaria pulcritud. Su ropa tenía
la virtud de no ajarse ni empolvarse nunca, y le caía sobre el
cuerpo como pintada' (XII, 1607). The doll image reduces the
Civil Servant mandarin to the level of a child.

g) *Children*

There are really two groups of children in *La de Bringas:*
the three Bringas children, accorded a significant space and
role in the novel, and their playmates, the Tellería, Lantigua,
Pez, and Sánchez Botín children, who are given appreciably
less space but who still fulfil the same important function of
mirroring the behaviour of their parents; Galdós calls attention
to this relationship in an important aside of the narrator's: 'No
miremos con indiferencia el retoñar de los caracteres humanos
en estos bosquejos de personas que llamamos niños. Ellos son
nuestras premisas; nosotros, ¿qué somos sino sus consecuen-
cias?' (XL, 1662-3). Round (*43*) has capably demonstrated how
the two younger Bringas children, Isabelita and Alfonsín, reflect the character traits of their father and mother respectively.
This aspect of the novel might be interpreted as proof of its
Naturalism: Isabelita's epileptic nightmares and her mania for

collecting things seem to be inherited from her father, Alfonsín's bustle, noise, excitement, from his mother. However, these family resemblances really form part of his already established pattern of mutually reflecting attitudes. The behaviour of the three Bringas children puts that of their parents into proper perspective, but so also does that of the Tellería and Pez children. Therefore, Galdós is not so much interested in demonstrating Naturalism's laws of heredity as in showing how the adult world is remarkably childlike and immature. The inevitable corollary of this parallel is that the children can also behave like adults. This point is very vividly made in the opening descriptions of these siblings (VI-VII, 1595-7; XIV, 1610). Some act the pedant, others, the adult lover:

> ¡María Santísima, lo que parecía aquella terraza! Había ninfas de traje alto que muy pronto iba a descender hasta el suelo, y otras de vestido bajo que dos semanas antes había sido alto. Las que acaban de recibir la investidura de mujeres se paseaban en grupos, cogidas del brazo, haciendo ensayos de formalidad y de conversación sosegada y discreta... Cuando por aquellas galerías conseguía deslizarse, con furtivo atrevimiento, algún novio agridulce, algún pollanco pretendiente, de bastoncito, corbata de color, hongo claro y tal vez pitillo en boquilla de ámbar..., ¡ay, Dios mío!, ¿quién podría contar las risas, los escondites, las sosadas, el juego inocente, la tontería deliciosa de aquellas frescas almas que acababan de abrir sus corolas al sol de la vida? Las breves cláusulas que ligeras se cruzaban eran, por un lado, lo más insulso del perfeccionado lenguaje social, y, por otro, el ingenuo balbucir de las sociedades primitivas. (VII, 1597)

If Pez, Francisco, Milagros and Rosalía revert to childhood at times, these pubescent children cannot wait to don the forms of adulthood and reproduce the empty social display of their parents. Galdós, whilst recognizing this as a natural progression, inevitably links it with the adult world of show that will be seen in the rest of the book: 'En todos estos casos se repite incesantemente el principio del Mundo, esto es, los pruritos de la Creación, el *querer ser*' (VII, 1597). None the less, they still retain some childhood habits: the girls, especially the buxom María Egipcíaca, greatly enjoy playing with the dolls (VII, 1598). The point is, of course, that like their elders, they combine, albeit in inverse proportions, infant and adult characteristics. The impression left with the reader is that there is not really much difference between child and adult in this world of the Palace, or indeed between human person and doll. This latter notion emerges very clearly from the initial description of Pez quoted above (p. 80), from Isabelita's first dream of the Palace dolls-house (VIII, 1600; crude drawings of dolls also appear on the walls of the servants' quarters, IV, 1592), and from another important aside by the narrator when commenting on the wonderful talking-doll sent by Agustín Caballero to Isabelita: 'de aquello a una criatura no había más que un paso: padecer' (VII, 1598).

h) *Dehumanization*

The doll imagery is just one of a number of devices Galdós uses to reduce the human dimensions of these characters. Another is animalization: Pez is the obvious example, but Francisco is also called 'el ratoncito Pérez' (XXXIII, 1648-9; XXXV, 1653; L, 1683); Vargas, a colleague in Francisco's office, appears as a flea in Isabelita's second dream (XXXIV, 1650-1); the narrator at the end considers Refugio a 'repugnante mosca' (L, 1683); Cándida clings to the Bringas family like a barnacle (XXVII, 1636); the guard who directs Pez and the narrator to Bringas's apartment in the first instance is a 'cancerbero con sombrero de tres picos' (III, 1591).

On the other hand, animals and objects are personified at times. The Palace pigeons are 'reinas indiscutidas e indiscutibles' (IV, 1593), obvious representations in figure, movements and final fate of both the fallen Queen and the surviving prostitutes like Rosalía, Milagros and Refugio. Francisco's hairpicture is appropriately personified when the doll-like Pez is looking at it: 'el maravilloso cristal tan poblado de pelos como humana cabeza, en algunas partes cabelludo, en otras claro, en todas como recién afeitado, gomoso, pegajoso, con brillo semejante al de las perfumadas pringues de tocador' (XVII, 1615).

Rosalía's dress-making models, like Agustín Caballero's talking doll, are very life-like: 'Sobre el sofá, media docena de figurines ostentaban en mentirosos colores esas damas imposibles, delgadas como juncos, tiesas como palos, cuyos pies son del tamaño de los dedos de la mano; damas que tienen por boca una oblea encarnada, que parecen vestidas de papel y se miran unas a otras con fisonomía de imbecilidad' (XV, 1612). Not only, then, are the distinctions between adults and youths blurred but so also are those between humans, animals and material objects; in the world created by Galdós in *La de Bringas* people and objects have lost, even exchanged, their proper identities.

The appearance of the word 'esperpento' on two occasions in *La de Bringas,* well before Valle-Inclán appropriated and popularized it, inevitably raises the question of the correspondence between the respective visions of Isabelline Spain.[35] For most of *La de Bringas* Rosalía and Francisco alternate between normal and abnormal human behaviour. But as the novel closes their redeeming traits of normality disappear to leave the caricaturesque outline that the other characters more readily reveal. It is only at this stage that Galdós's two major characters join hands with Valle's dehumanized puppets.[36] But then a uniformly 'esperpento' characterization would be inconsistent with the basic perspectivism of *La de Bringas.* Outside labels, like the inner language of the novel, can be deceptive.

---

[35] V. A. Smith and J. E. Varey, ' "Esperpento": Some Early Usages in the Novels of Galdós', in *Galdós Studies,* ed. J. E. Varey (London: Tamesis, 1970), pp. 195-204 (at pp. 197-9).

[36] José Amor y Vázquez, 'Galdós, Valle-Inclán, esperpento', in *Actas del Primer Congreso Internacional de Estudios Galdosianos* (Las Palmas: Excmo. Cabildo Insular de Gran Canaria, 1977), pp. 189-200, comprehensively reviews previous studies on the similarities between the works of Galdós and Valle.

9. The uses of language

IN Galdós's indictment of Isabelline society, the language
spoken by the characters and the words chosen by the narrator are very important weapons. As if to direct our attention
to that importance, Galdós shows how words play a part in the
development of the events: Pez's empty rhetoric is used to
great effect in the seduction and, fittingly, in the abandonment
of Rosalía (XVI, 1613; XXV, 1631-2; XXXII, 1646; XXXV,
1653; XLIV, 1669-70). Language is also an important defensive
weapon for Rosalía to explain her purchase of the shawl or
the family's enforced stay in Madrid during the summer
(XXXVIII, 1659). The snob appeal of the name Arcachon also
plays a great part in her surprising willingness to accept Agustín
Caballero's invitation: 'Ya se había acostumbrado a la idea
de...darles [a sus amigas] con Arcachón en los hocicos, de
poner en sus cartas la data de Arcachón, y por fin, de arca-
chonizarse para todo el otoño e invierno próximos' (XXXIX,
1662). Hence it is not altogether unexpected that Rosalía's
greatest humiliation should be due to the enunciation of the
dreaded stigma 'cursi': 'Aquella frase la hería en lo más vivo
de su alma' (XLVIII, 1678). The single word has such a devas-
tating effect upon Rosalía because it publicizes to the world her
inability to close the gap between reality and appearances, her
constant struggle throughout the book. [37] It is the one word of
sordid reality that is anathema to this social group; for them
language is normally a reassuring refuge, an effective means to
hide the inner vacuity, as the solecisms of General Pedro Minio
(VI, 1596), the newspaper accounts of Milagros's soirée (XXIII,

[37] Enrique Tierno Galván, 'Aparición y desarrollo de nuevas pers-
pectivas de valoración social en el siglo XIX: lo cursi', *Revista de Estudios Políticos*, 62 (March-April, 1952), 85-106, and Ramón Gómez de
la Serna, *Lo cursi y otros ensayos* (Buenos Aires: Sudamericana, 1943),
pp. 7-54, offer comprehensive studies of 'cursilería'.

1628), and the preposterous names given to the Royal enclosures in the Retiro (XVI, 1613) and the Manzanares swimming establishments (XXXVIII, 1658) show clearly enough. At times an underlying coarseness of language surfaces to reveal their empty pretentiousness: Tula calls her husband 'una bestia condecorada' (VI, 1596), and Francisco is elated by Milagros's news of the Generals' arrest: 'luego dicen que Ibrahim [González Bravo] está ido: lo que está es más despabilado que nunca, grandísimos pillos' (XXX, 1642).

The narrator's own careful attention to the selection of his language also contributes to the effective ridiculing of these characters. We can notice his deliberation when he considers the appropriate description for Milagros's melodramatic behaviour: 'Dicho esto, le entró una congoja y una convulsioncilla de estas que las mujeres llaman ataque de nervios, por llamarlo de alguna manera, seguida de un espasmo de los que reciben el bonito nombre de síncope' (XXIII, 1629). The exaggerated pathos of Romanticism is in fact used for great effect to deflate the seriousness of some apparently tragic situations in which Rosalía and Francisco find themselves: when Rosalía is concerned about the repayment of her first loan, 'el bueno de Gonzalo [Torres] la tranquilizó [a Rosalía] al momento. ¡Qué pronto volvieron las rosas, para hablar a lo poético, al demudado rostro de la dama!' (XI, 1605). When she rushes in to see her husband after the initial attack of blindness, she finds Francisco rubbing his eyes: 'los volvió a abrir, y moviendo mucho los párpados, como los poetas cuando leen sus versos, exclamó con acento que desgarraba: —¡No veo! ... ¡No veo!' (XX, 1621).

As with his optical references and his structuring of scenes, Galdós also manages to create ironic references or reprises through the multiple meanings of individual words and phrases repeated at intervals throughout the novel. Francisco's matronymic is Caballero: this is the term applied to the angel in the hair-picture, to Pez (by Rosalía, XLIV, 1671), to Refugio's unidentified male friend, and finally to the militia guards who take control of the Palace (XLIX, 1682). The multiple irony (for the designation is hardly appropriate in any of the instances) reinforces the discrepancy between the appearances and

reality of this society. Other examples are not so extensive.
Agustín's invitation upsets Rosalía but 'en la tempestad de
nubarrones que se desató en su cerebro brillaban relámpagos
que decían: "¡Arcachón!"' (XXXIX, 1660). This metaphorical
thunder and lightning recall the real meteorological phenomena
of the Madrid summer that had irritated Rosalía so much only
a short while before, at the end of the preceding chapter
(XXXVIII, 1659). Similarly, in her second dream, Isabelita
recalls her father's conversation with Pez about the forthcoming
Revolution and the rivers of blood that will flow in the streets;
the realistic counterpoint is sounded when at the end of the
nightmare she vomits: 'allá fue todo fuera como un torrente'
(XXXIV, 1651). After describing Milagros's ostentatious church
service in gastronomical terms ('[Rosalía] oyó sermón patético,
aflautado, un guisote de lugares comunes con salsa de gestos
de teatro', XVIII, 1617), the narrator reports that Rosalía,
'mártir de los insufribles métodos de su marido', has to rush
home to prepare his dinner. Thus religious image replaces
religious reality, and gastronomic reality replaces gastronomic
image. The inevitable result is that both functions are equalized
with a corresponding inversion of values: Milagros's external
display of religion is empty and materialistic, whilst Francisco's
true religion is his physical or material well-being. In the final
chapter of the novel Rosalía's 'mudanza moral' is underlined
in the following paragraph by the physical 'mudanzas' or household removals of some Palace servants *(43)*.

Because of their contextual incongruity individual religious
references provide a frequent source of humour: the picture
that Rosalía has of Torres asking for his money is imprinted on
her mind like the 'Inri' on the Cross of Jesus (XIX, 1620). For
Rosalía, Refugio is less objectionable when she notices her
cousin's surprising display of new clothes: 'Así como el Espíritu Santo, bajando a los labios del pecador arrepentido, puede
santificar a éste, Refugio, a los ojos de su ilustre pariente, se
redimía por la divinidad de su discurso' (XXVI, 1635). Milagros is overjoyed to receive the unexpected loan from Rosalía:
'Los que han tenido la dicha de ver, ora realmente, ora en
extática figuración, el Cielo abierto y en él las cohortes de
ángeles voladores cantando las alabanzas del Señor, no ponen,

de seguro, una cara más radiante que la que puso Milagros
al oír aquel venturoso anuncio' (XXXI, 1645). This contrast
between the image and reality of the Isabelline world is reduc-
ed to its smallest linguistic format in the oxymorons that appear
in the novel. The 'real república' of the servants' quarters (III,
1591) is an obvious example, but the device is repeated on a
number of other occasions: the hair-picture contains 'girasoles
chiquitos, pensamientos grandes' (XVII, 1616); Cándida and
Francisco talk of 'negocios altos y ... política baja' (XIX, 1621).
Though delighted with the possibility of Francisco's recovery
of eyesight, Rosalía is also anxious lest he discover her pawn-
ing of the candelabra: 'se hallaba en una perplejidad harto
dolorosa. La expresaba diciéndose que tal vez se alegraría
de no estar tan alegre' (XXV, 1633).

The one unmistakable result of this careful use of ironic
language to point the gap between image and reality is a
consistently comic tone to which structure and characterization,
naturally, also contribute *(17)*. [38] Some critics *(22, 41)* have
tended to see this element of comedy as an instrument of moral
criticism. There is no doubt that most of Galdós's novels do
convey a general moral lesson, but in *La de Bringas* this purpose is explicitly built into the text. The story of Rosalía's fall
receives its moral commentary when Refugio gives Rosalía
'un buen consejo ...: es que no ande en líos con doña Milagros, que es capaz de volver del revés a la más sentada. Métase
en su rincón, *a la vera* del pisahormigas, y déjese de historias
... No vaya más a casa de Sobrino y créame. Es mucho Madrid
éste. No se fíe de los carañitos de la Tellería, que es muy
ladina y muy cuca' (XLVIII, 1677-8). From the outset, Galdós
presents Rosalía's passion for clothes in religious-moral terms:
'Su antigua modestia, que más tenía de necesidad que de virtud,
fue sometida a una prueba de la que no salió victoriosa. En
otro tiempo, la prudencia de Thiers pudo poner un freno a

---

[38] For a discussion of the different categories of irony, see also D. C.
Muecke, *The Compass of Irony* (London: Methuen, 1969). Henri
Bergson, 'Laughter', in *Comedy*, ed. Wylie Sypher (Garden City, New
York: Doubleday, 1956), pp. 59-190, makes some pertinent observations
on the comic use of words (at pp. 127-45).

los apetitos de lujo, haciéndonos creer a todos que no exis-
tían, cuando lo único positivo en esto era la imposibilidad de
satisfacerlos. Es el incidente primordial de la historia humana,
y el caso eterno, el caso de los casos en orden de fragilidad'
(IX, 1601). At other times the narrator's commentary can be
more directly bitter when, for example, he describes the Maundy Thursday ceremony in the Palace ('la farsa de aquel cuadro
teatral', VIII, 1599) or the grotesque style of the Retiro archi-
tecture ('tontería pura', XVI, 1613).

And yet this overt moralizing tone strikes the reader as
being too exaggerated to be completely true, especially when in
the closing lines of the novel the narrator declares: 'no me
creía yo en el caso de serlo [sostén de la cesante familia] contra
todos los fueros de la moral y de la economía doméstica' (L,
1683). These words jar uneasily with his record of other events
in the same chapter. The question immediately arises then:
is the narrator as guilty as his characters in using language to
conceal the truth about his own actions and thoughts? Does
the language of humour include the narrator as well? Is the
narrator no more than another actor in the story?

10. *The narrator*

THE anonymous narrator of *La de Bringas* is very conscious
of his rôle as a story-teller: he reminds the reader of
previous developments (XIII, 1607); he anticipates future events
(XVII, 1614); he omits or abbreviates details for the reader's
benefit (XXIII, 1628) as well as adding personal assessments
and moral commentaries. In short, in his brief, though persis-
tent, authorial interventions, the narrator is asserting the cus-
tomary textual authority and control of the omniscient narrator.
The occasional shortcomings when, for instance, he is unsure
of the exact date of Rosalía's lie to Francisco about the shawl
(XI, 1604), or baffled by Milagros's requests for money after
her successful soirée (XXIX, 1641), or unable to explain the
reasons for Rosalía's blatant display of new clothes before
her husband (XLVIII, 1678), give this omniscience an appropriate leaven of human fallibility.

However, the narrator is also an actor in his own story. His
participation is not limited, as in *Tormento,* to a brief acknowl-
edgement of friendship with his characters that authenticates
the fiction, giving it an appearance of historical documentation
(this is, though, the purpose of his brief reference to sighting
Pez and Rosalía on their walks in the Retiro, XVI, 1613). The
role he gives himself on other occasions is far more significant,
especially at the important points of the novel's beginning and
ending. His visit to the Palace with Pez serves to start the story
and introduce the reader to this fantastic setting. But at the
same time it also reveals the narrator's own rather enigmatic
character. He has never before visited the Palace but is none
the less determined, like Pez, to press ahead without the help
of a guide until they reach Bringas's apartment: 'La idea de
perdernos no nos contrariaba mucho; porque saboreábamos
de antemano el gusto de salir al fin a puerto sin auxilio de
práctico y por virtud de nuestro propio instinto topográfico. El

laberinto nos atraía' (IV, 1592). More significant perhaps than
this practical recklessness is the reason for the narrator's visit:
to ask Francisco the favour of stopping legal proceedings
brought by a Palace official over an obviously shady land
purchase that the narrator has recently made. Pez introduces
the narrator to Bringas because he in turn owes the narrator
some (unspecified) favours. The narrator's corresponding gift
to Francisco in October clearly shows, in retrospect, that the
narrator is a willing participant in the Isabelline system of
deals, favours and personal recommendations at the expense
of justice and probity. Far from dispelling the reader's interest
in his character as he had hoped ('pero antes de seguir, quiero
quitar de esta relación el estorbo de mi personalidad, lo que
lograré explicando en breves palabras el objeto de mi visita al
señor de Bringas', VI, 1595), the narrator's semi-obscure ex-
planation only serves to increase that interest, ensuring that his
subsequent appearances and comments are not accepted totally
without hesitation.

The narrator's visit to the Palace takes place in March 1868.
His present to Francisco, anticipated out of chronological order
as we saw above (pp. 47-8), is in October of the same year, the
period covered in the novel's final chapter when the narrator
again assumes a prominent rôle in the development of events.
To the reader's great surprise, this friend of the monarchists
Bringas and Tula has now been appointed Administrator of
the Palace by the Revolutionary Junta. Not only are the reasons
for this political appointment surprisingly vague but so also
is the narrator's method of disclosing the news. He first notes
that the Junta took control of the Palace in good order, 'nom-
brando quien lo custodiase' (L, 1682). Two long sentences later
he slyly reveals: 'Tuve ocasión de conocer y apreciar los sen-
timientos de cada uno de los habitantes de la ciudad en este
particular, *porque mi suerte o mi desgracia quiso que fuese yo
el designado* por la Junta para custodiar el coloso y administrar
todo lo que había pertenecido a la Corona' (my italics; L,
1682). Luck, chance, which the narrator would prefer to call
'Filosofía de la Historia' (L, 1683), has been the guiding prin-
ciple in one form or another (coincidence, fantasy, whim) of

this Palace structure, the characters' actions and the events of the novel as they have unfolded. It is highly appropriate that chance should now govern the narrator's final adventure. The position as administrator is highly ironic in view of the fact that his initial visit to the Palace with Pez was due to 'ciertos dimes y diretes con un administradorcillo de la Casa Real' (VI, 1595), and also because of the frequency with which he has throughout the novel referred to the phantom administrators of Cándida and Milagros (e.g. XI, 1605; XXIII, 1629). Moreover in the performance of his duties, the narrator shows himself to be like his great friend Pez, for whom 'la Administración era una tapadera de fórmulas baldías, creada para encubrir el sistema práctico del favor personal, cuya clave está en el cohecho y las recomendaciones' (XII, 1607):

> Desde que me instalé en mi oficina faltábame tiempo para oír a los vecinos angustiados de la ciudad. A algunos, por razón de su cargo, no había más remedio que dejarlos, pues ellos solos conocían ciertos pormenores administrativos que debían conservarse. En este caso estaban los guardamuebles y la guardarropa. Otros exponían sutiles razones para no salir, y no faltó quien alegase méritos revolucionarios para ser inquilino de la Nación, como antes lo habían sido de la Monarquía. Todos traían cartas de recomendación de diferentes personajes caídos o por caer, levantados o por levantar, pidiendo con ellas, o bien alojamiento perpetuo, o bien prórroga para mudarse. (L, 1682)

The narrator's readiness to surrender political principles to personal convenience (the contrast 'personajes caídos o por caer, levantados o por levantar' is an apt reminder of Isabelita's dolls-house vision of the Palace) is well illustrated by his reaction to Cándida's absurdly long petition. His readiness to compromise moral principles is the plot's final surprise. The narrator seems to have three private meetings with Rosalía in which the economic needs of the family are made clear to him. On the second occasion, he cryptically reports that Rosalía looked at him during the interview with 'miradas un tanto flamígeras' (L, 1683). The next time he again mysteriously

reports: 'Estábamos en plena época revolucionaria. Quiso re-
petir las pruebas de su ruinosa amistad, mas yo me apresuré
a ponerles punto, pues si parecía natural que ella fuese el sostén
de la cesante familia, no me creía yo en el caso de serlo, contra
todos los fueros de la moral y de la economía doméstica' (L,
1683). The obvious implication is that the narrator has also
had, like Pez, sexual relations with Rosalía at their second
meeting (the narrator could also be Refugio's 'un caballero que
yo conozco') and that Rosalía now tries to repeat the seduction,
but the narrator, realizing the dangers, ends the liaison. The
October birthday present for Francisco can only now be appreciated at its full value: it is a disguised payment for sexual
favours. In his moral behaviour the narrator is as corrupt and
hypocritical as the other characters whom he is so ready to
ridicule and criticize. The narrator's concealment of the truth
about his own position is all the more difficult to perceive until
the end because he controls the substance and form of his nar-
ration. When the truth does emerge, it is characteristically
concealed by the rhetoric of fiction.

Our narrator is indeed Booth's unreliable narrator. [39] This
rôle is represented emblematically in his behaviour at Tula's
soporific tertulia when he only half sees and half hears the
surrounding scene. It is appropriate, then, that Galdós should
associate this narrator of *La de Bringas* with another equally
enigmatic narrator, Máximo Manso (V, 1594; VI, 1595; XXI,
1624).

Galdós succeeds in investing his novel with a perplexing
jacket that is consonant with the ambiguous perspectives generated at all levels by the interior fiction. But if the novel could
be neatly parcelled up in this manner, it would belie its basic
texture. Hence it is not without significance that some critics
have tried in varying degrees to see in our unnamed, unreliable
narrator a representation of Galdós himself (*16,* p. 125; *26,*
p. 444; *28,* p. 601; *40,* p. 340), or the fictional Ido del Sagrario
(*32,* pp. 59-60), or the historical figure who was appointed

---

[39] Wayne C. Booth, *The Rhetoric of Fiction* (Chicago: University
of Chicago Press, 1961), pp. 158-9.

Administrator of the Palace after the 1868 Revolution. [40] But the identity of the narrator/author is only the second side of the triangle of fictional creation. We must now look at the final side: that which represents the reader's contribution.

---

[40] In actual fact, a ten-man commission was appointed by the Revolutionary Government as legal guardians of the Palace; see Laureano López Rodó, *El patrimonio nacional* (Madrid: Consejo Superior de Investigaciones Científicas, 1954), pp. 205-6.

11. *Conclusion*

THE penultimate layer of illusion in *La de Bringas* involves the reader who may believe that this fictional experience of the Bringas circle has no relation to his or her own world. However, the first words of the novel ('Era aquello ..., ¿cómo lo diré yo?', I, 1587) imply that the narrator is also involving the reader in his fictional world, as we saw in Chapter 2, and, consequently, in its process of self-deception.[41] This notion is confirmed a short while later in the same chapter when the narrator addresses the reader directing his/her attention towards details in the hair-picture: 'reparad en lo nimio, escrupuloso, y firme de tan difícil trabajo' (I, 1587). This is, of course, a common literary device which Galdós and other novelists often used to involve the reader. The danger is that the reader ignores the address because of its repeated use in fiction. Here again the fundamental ambiguity and the ever-deepening perspectives of *La de Bringas* are at work: Galdós does intend the address to be taken seriously by the reader at one level (that is: the reader of *La de Bringas*, despite his/her distance from outside the fiction, is involved in the recreation of the perplexing experience) but at another level, because it is such a literary cliché, he is also accepting the possibility that the reader will ignore it.

One final layer of illusion remains to be dispelled: to the reader of which century or year is Galdós directing *La de Bringas*? In all of the preceding novels of the 'serie contemporánea' he had very carefully made the juncture between the time period of his story and that of his contemporary audience. One example of the 'doble visión', from *Tormento*, will suffice:

---

[41] Eamonn J. Rodgers, in the introduction to his edition of *Tormento* (Oxford: Pergamon Press, 1977), pp. 12-13, makes the same point in relation to that novel.

the narrator comments early in the novel: 'En una Sociedad como aquélla [i.e. of 1867], o como ésta [i.e. of 1883], pues la variación en diez y seis años no ha sido muy grande ...' (IV, 1480). In *La de Bringas* Galdós avoids (rather surprisingly) any such parallels. In this way the novel's appeal can transcend its immediate socio-historical context, as several critics have noted (see p. 17 above). In those materialist societies in which a total absence of moral values is often covered up by a glittering exterior, and a dangerous, uncontrollable imagination predominates over a sober realization of the reality of life, the relevance of *La de Bringas* is indeed appreciable: the vanity of the social game of appearances is exposed, not directly by a moral prosecutor, but indirectly, by an unsuspecting fellow sinner.

In his brilliant control of the great variety of detail and its ordering in *La de Bringas* (a sustained control perhaps unequalled in any other of his novels), Galdós has succeeded in constructing a story in which every aspect reflects to some extent the ambiguous perspectives established by his initial image of the hair-picture; or, to adapt the phrase Rosalía uses to describe her husband's concept of dress-making, Galdós has achieved 'las metamorfosis de un mismo vestido hasta lo infinito' (XXV, 1632). In the structure of this Guide, I have attempted to imitate that gradual unfolding of multiple layers of meaning that is *La de Bringas*'s extraordinary richness. However, this study would be untrue to its subject if it claimed a definitive interpretation. It is only one of a long succession of monographs, many brilliant. More will follow as further layers of meaning are peeled off this masterpiece of Galdós.

Bibliographical Note

A. BIBLIOGRAPHIES

For details of the editions of Galdós's works, see Miguel Hernández Suárez, *Bibliografía de Galdós*, I (Las Palmas: Excmo. Cabildo Insular, 1972).

For further critical studies see: Theodore A. Sackett, *Pérez Galdós: an Annotated Bibliography* (Albuquerque: University of New Mexico Press, 1968); Hensley C. Woodbridge, *Benito Pérez Galdós: a Selective Annotated Bibliography* (Metuchen, N. J.: Scarecrow Press, 1975); J. E. Varey, 'Galdós in the Light of Recent Criticism', in *Galdós Studies*, ed. J. E. Varey (London: Tamesis, 1970), pp. 1-35; Luciano García Lorenzo, 'Bibliografía galdosiana", *CHA*, LXXXIV (1970-1), 758-97; Miguel Hernández Suárez, 'Bibliografía', *AG*, III (1968), 191-212; IV (1969), 127-52; VI (1971), 139-63; VII (1972), 145-65; IX (1974), 175-206.

B. HISTORICAL BACKGROUND

1. Raymond Carr, *Spain 1808-1939* (Oxford: Clarendon Press, 1966). The standard analysis of the main currents and developments of the period.

2. Francis Gribble, *The Tragedy of Isabella II* (London: Chapman and Hall, 1913). Still the only study in English; mostly anecdotal and descriptive rather than analytical.

3. Clara E. Lida and Iris M. Zavala, eds, *La revolución de 1868: historia, pensamiento, literatura* (New York: Las Américas, 1970). Useful collection of recent essays.

C. BIOGRAPHIES

4. Joaquín Casalduero, *Vida y obra de Benito Pérez Galdós (1843-1920)*, 3rd ed. (Madrid: Gredos, 1970). Although brief on biography, his schematized interpretation of the works has been very influential.

5. H. Chonon Berkowitz, *Pérez Galdós: Spanish Liberal Crusader* (Madison: University of Wisconsin Press, 1948). Still the only comprehensive biography; unfortunately vitiated by imprecision and conjecture.

6. Walter T. Pattison, *Benito Pérez Galdós,* Twayne's World Authors Series, 341 (Boston: Twayne, 1975). Incorporates recent biographical, even if not literary, research.

D. GALDÓS ON THE NOVEL

7. *Ensayos de crítica literaria,* ed. Laureano Bonet (Barcelona: Península, 1972). Contains the most important theoretical statements, with a good introduction.
8. William H. Shoemaker, ed. *Los prólogos de Galdós* (Urbana: University of Illinois Press, 1962). A useful, though incomplete, collection.

E. GENERAL WORKS

9. Rodolfo Cardona, 'Galdós and Realism', in *Galdós (Papers Read at the Modern Foreign Language Department Symposium: Nineteenth-Century Spanish Literature: Benito Pérez Galdós)* (Fredericksburg, Virginia: Mary Washington College of the University of Virginia, 1967), pp. 71-94. Illustrates the general problem of classifying Galdós as a Realist with a fine study of the function of the hair-picture in *LB*.
10. Gustavo Correa, *Realidad, ficción y símbolo en las novelas de Pérez Galdós: ensayo de estética realista* (Bogotá: Instituto Caro y Cuervo, 1967). An interesting attempt to explain Galdós's realism.
11. Kay Engler, *The Structure of Realism: the 'Novelas contemporáneas' of Benito Pérez Galdós,* University of North Carolina Studies in Romance Languages and Literatures, 184 (Chapel Hill: University of North Carolina Press, 1977). Applies some modern theories of Realism to some of Galdós's novels; *LB* is not accorded much attention.
12. Sherman H. Eoff, *The Novels of Pérez Galdós: the Concept of Life as Dynamic Process* (St Louis: Washington University, 1954). An early schematic survey, spoiled by a confusing style.
13. Ricardo Gullón, *Galdós, novelista moderno* (Madrid: Gredos, 1966). A provocative study.
14. ———, *Técnicas de Galdós* (Madrid: Taurus, 1970). A collection of earlier articles. Pp. 103-34: includes those on *LB (21, 36, 37).*
15. Hans Hinterhäuser, *Los 'Episodios nacionales' de Benito Pérez Galdós* (Madrid: Gredos, 1963). The standard work on the *episodios* but very few references to *LB*.
16. José F. Montesinos, *Galdós,* 3 vols (Madrid: Castalia, 1968-73). Despite its ponderous style, a panoramic view full of insights. II (1969), pp. 120-52 for *LB*.
17. Michael Nimetz, *Humor in Galdós: a Study of the 'Novelas contemporáneas'* (New Haven: Yale University Press, 1968). The best study so far; attempts to classify the types of humour in Galdós's novels.

18. Marie-Claire Petit, *Les Personnages féminins dans les romans de Benito Pérez Galdós* (Lyon: Université de Lyon, 1972). An over-schematized catalogue of feminist themes and aspects.

19. Antonio Regalado García, *Benito Pérez Galdós y la novela histórica española: 1868-1912* (Madrid: Ínsula, 1966). A controversial recent assessment of Galdós's historical novel, with little to say on *LB*.

20. Joseph Schraibman, *Dreams in the Novels of Galdós* (New York: Hispanic Institute, 1969). A detailed catalogue.

F. EDITIONS (see also Preface)

21. Ricardo Gullón (Englewood Cliffs, N. J.: Prentice-Hall, 1967). Takes some minor liberties with the text but is the best edition available because of its extensive footnotes and perceptive introduction which studies Galdós's life and works in general and then concentrates on certain aspects of *LB* entitled: 'Historia y novela; el maleficio mesocrático; caos y laberinto; el autor-personaje; la verdad en el sueño; el lenguaje.'

22. *The Spendthrifts*, trans. Gamel Woolsey with introd. by Gerald Brenan (New York: Farrar Strauss and Young, 1952; also pub. in Great Britain by the New English Library in the Four Square Classics, 1962). A fluent translation but also contains some surprising errors and omissions. A typically perceptive introduction by Brenan (pp. 7-12).

G. CONTEMPORARY REVIEWS

23. Leopoldo Alas, *Galdós* (Madrid: Renacimiento, 1912), pp. 135-6. Unavoidably short, but favourable.

24. Luis Alfonso, *'La de Bringas'*, *La Época* (2 July 1884), p. 3. Very negative.

25. Cristóbal Botella, 'La semana', *El Noticiero* (13 October 1884), p. 3. Very brief and unfavourable.

26. Orlando, 'Novelas españolas del año literario', *Revista de España*, C (1884), 430-48. An in-depth review of Galdós's achievements to date. Very hostile, however, to *LB*.

27. Jacinto Octavio Picón, *'La de Bringas'*, *El Imparcial* (14 July 1884), p. 1. Very favourable.

28. Léo Quesnel, 'Littérature espagnole contemporaine (1): M. Benito Pérez Galdós', *Revue Politique et Littéraire*, XXXV (1885), 598-602. Contains some perceptive observations as well as remarkable errors of interpretation.

H. 'LA DE BRINGAS' AND 'TORMENTO'

29. P. A. Bly, 'From Disorder to Order: the Pattern of "arreglar" References in Galdós's *Tormento* and *La de Bringas'*, *Neophilologus*, LXII (1978), 392-405.

30. David Cluff, 'The Structure and Meaning of Galdós' *Tormento'*, *Reflexión* 2, III-IV (1974-5), 159-67. Concentrates on *Tormento* but points out some correspondences with *LB*.

31. Robert M. Fedorchek, 'Rosalía and the Rhetoric of Dialogue in Galdós's *Tormento* and *La de Bringas'*, *Revista de Estudios Hispánicos*, XII (1978), 199-216. Makes the obvious point that Rosalía's language reveals her character.

32. Robert Ricard, 'Place et signification de *Tormento* entre *El doctor Centeno* et *La de Bringas'*, in *Aspects de Galdós* (Paris: Presses Universitaires de France, 1963), pp. 44-60. An important study of the relationship between the two novels.

I. ARTICLES ON 'LA DE BRINGAS'

33. Andrés Amorós, 'El ambiente de *La de Bringas'*, *Reales Sitios*, VI (1965), 61-8. A perceptive analysis, with helpful photos, of the rôle of the Palace.

34. P. A. Bly, 'The Use of Distance in Galdós's *La de Bringas'*, *Modern Language Review*, LXIX (1974), 88-97.

35. George D. J. Edberg, 'Un estudio de don Manuel del Pez, una creación literaria galdosiana', *Humanitas*, XI (1961), 407-17. A catalogue of character traits as displayed in *LB* and other novels.

36. Ricardo Gullón, 'Claves de Galdós', *In*, 284-5 (July-August, 1970), 8. Two sections ('estructura' and 'espacio') added to his introduction to the edition *(21)*; later collected in *14*.

37. ———, 'Introducción a *La de Bringas'*, *In*, 238 (September, 1966), 1, 12. A preview of three sections ('el maleficio mesocrático', 'caos y laberinto' and 'el autor-personaje') which he later published in the introduction to his ed. *(21)*.

38. Jennifer Lowe, 'Galdós' Presentation of Rosalía in *La de Bringas'*, *Hispanófila*, 50 (January, 1974), 49-65. An excellent analysis that focusses mainly on Rosalía's relationship with Pez.

39. Pedro Ortiz Armengol, 'Tres apuntes hacia temas de *Fortunata y Jacinta'*, *Letras de Deusto*, IV (1974), 241-59. Pp. 241-51 include an examination of Galdós's use of both the historical and fictional Francisco Bringas.

40. Julian Palley, 'Aspectos de *La de Bringas'*, *Kentucky Romance Quarterly*, XV (1969), 339-48. An interesting review of several features: 'la obra de pelo; el punto de vista; burocracia y laberinto; *La de Bringas* y *Madame Bovary*; La Gloriosa y la ce-

guera; La Comida de los Pobres; la crisis: Rosalía y Refugio; el laberinto, patetismo e ironía.'

41. V. S. Pritchett, 'Galdós', in *Books in General* (London: Chatto and Windus, 1953), pp. 31-6. An accurate assessment of *LB*'s merits.

41a. Arthur Ramírez, 'The Heraldic Emblematic Image in Galdós's *La de Bringas*', *Revista de Estudios Hispánicos*, XIV (1980), 65-74. Following Gullón, he offers occasional good insights into the function of the opening hairwork description.

42. Suzanne Raphael, '*La de Bringas*: ¿*La de todos*?', in *Hommage à André Joucla-Ruau* (Aix-en-Provence: Université de Provence, 1974), pp. 196-206. She sees echoes of Quevedo's *Sueños* in Isabelita's first dream.

43. Nicholas G. Round, 'Rosalía Bringas' Children', *AG*, VI (1971), 43-50. A cogent analysis of the presentation of the two children in Chapter XL of *LB*.

44. Roberto G. Sánchez, 'The Function of Dates and Deadlines in Galdós' *La de Bringas*', *HR*, XLVI (1978), 299-311. An excellent, though still incomplete, study.

45. William H. Shoemaker, 'Galdós' Classical Scene in *La de Bringas*', *HR*, XXVII (1959), 423-34; also reprinted in his *Estudios sobre Galdós* (Valencia: Castalia, 1970). Disappointing in that it concentrates on source-hunting rather than analysis.

46. J. E. Varey, 'Francisco Bringas, "nuestro buen Thiers"', *AG*, I (1966), 63-9. A fluent, absorbing study of the ironic use that Galdós makes of Thiers's economic theories.

47. Chad C. Wright, 'Imagery of Light and Darkness in *La de Bringas*', *AG*, XIII (1978), 5-12. A partial, though occasionally perceptive, treatment of this important motif.